BOOKS BY BRYAN MACMAHON

Novels:
Children of the Rainbow
The Honey Spike

Short Stories:
The Lion Tamer
The Red Petticoat

Travel:
Here's Ireland

Children's Stories:
Jack O'Moora and the King of Ireland's Son
Brendan of Ireland (with S. Suschitzky)
Patsy-o and His Wonderful Pets

Peig

Peig

The Autobiography of

Peig Sayers
of the Great Blasket Island

Translated into English by
BRYAN MacMAHON

Introduction by Eoin McKiernan

Illustrations by Catriona O'Connor

Syracuse University Press   1974

First Published 1973 by The Talbot Press, Dublin

Copyright © 1973 by Bryan MacMahon

Copyright © 1974 by Syracuse University Press

Syracuse, New York

Library of Congress Cataloging in Publication Data

Sayers, Peig.
  Peig: the autobiography of Peig Sayers of the Great Blasket
Island.

  1. Sayers, Peig. 2. Blasket Islands, Ire.
DA990.B65S4213   1974   914.19′6′0380924 [B]
ISBN 0-8156-0106-9   74-11721

Manufactured in the United States of America

INTRODUCTION TO AMERICAN EDITION

Homo sum: humani nihil a me alienum puto

In the bayous of literature rest many books whose humanity occasionally recalls them to the mainstream of thought. *Peig* is one such. In books such as these the quality of honesty and sincerity, of life lived at the bone, is the conduit through which the thought of one generation passes to illuminate the problems of another age or place. The reader's discovery is the more jolting when he recognizes that the writer had not consciously attempted to foresee the problem of the later generation. It may be a tendentious digression to pursue this point but no one doubts that poverty, reticulated with the other great questions of war, health, happiness—and with the ultimate philosophical question about life, *why?*—is the most urgent problem of our century.

In this connection it is interesting to observe how closely some of today's sociologists are approaching the "prime matter" of literature itself. Extended questionnaires, anecdotal observations, various apperception devices, tape recordings, lengthy shared cultural experiences have combined to elevate the intuitive aspects of investigation to something more than what yesterday would have accepted as "scientific." In our search for solutions to basic human problems the annals of the poor have assumed a new importance.

If Robert Coles and Oscar Lewis, fine sociologists that they are, can tape record and otherwise annotate the lives of the poor in the search for common etiological factors in poverty, what scholar will take the next step of analyzing and correlating the basic constituents of the autobiographies of the poor? What an opportunity to discover whether an analysis of the autobiography of

1

poverty could reveal common themes, attitudes, responses, mechanisms of adjustment, and so on. One is reminded of this potential, for example, by the relevation in concentration camp autobiographies of unappreciated—or forgotten—dynamics of human response. In brief, if there is validity in the study of the lengthy taped responses of the poor to questions posed by the interviewer, might there not also be validity in the study of the response to life as a whole as written by one who endured the poverty, who recorded it as an element, but whose concern was not the poverty itself?

Two books in this genre, neither attempting to be a report on poverty yet each a vivid account of what it meant to be poor, recommend themselves to such a study: this one, the autobiography of an Irish woman who lived her whole life on the ragged edge of the westernmost frontier of Europe, the Corcaguiney Peninsula and the Great Blasket Island, and the other, the memoirs of an American backwoodsman who grew up on the ragged edge of the Adirondack Mountains wilderness.* Peig Sayers of County Kerry and Henry Conklin of New York State shared not only poverty, hardship, deprivation, and sorrow; they also shared an indomitable, optimistic spirit which surmounted not only their individual distresses but also the differences in time, space, culture, religion, sex, economy, and language which characterized their lives. Though both were often dismayed, neither writer was overwhelmed by overwhelming conditions. Why not?

One may well object that it is irreverent if not crass to approach books like *Peig* in so functional a manner. One's only defense would be that, while one does not have to see *Peig* as primarily the raw material for sociological

---

* *Through "Poverty's Vale": A Hardscrabble Boyhood in Upstate New York, 1832–1862*, by Henry Conklin, edited by Wendell Tripp, copyright © 1974 by Syracuse University Press.

analyses, one cannot overlook its testimonial value in this respect, all the more coercive since it is an unconscious commentary upon the condition.

But *Peig* is, first and last, the song of life. Delight, buoyancy of spirit, hope, joy, courage, faith in humanity —these are the chief products of a reading of *Peig*. We come away from her book refreshed and purified, knowing that rare as she was, she lives also as Everywoman. Born into a tiny island community with roots in European prehistory, she reappears in other guises, in other ages, in other places. If the comparison is not too precious, one might say she is the incarnation of the goddess figure, stripped to its mythical essence. O'Casey's Juno, for example, is the better understood by one's acquaintance with Peig; so, too, is Maurya in *Riders to the Sea*. Peig is elemental humanity—stoic, not grim; buoyant, not giddy; fated, but free.

In her late troubled years dictating her autobiography to her poet-son—first having been persuaded that her "uneventful" life could be of interest to others—she evinces no self-pity but a quiet knowledge of the heroic, almost mythic, quality of life as she knew it: "but people like us will never again be there."

Her home, after her marriage, was on the Great Blasket Island (surely the people who called so small a lump of rock *great* saw their own small society in mythic terms!) —the westernmost thrust of inhabited Europe. (Before the end of her life America was to become as near to these people—through emigration—as the mainland, only two miles across the sound in which a ship of Spain's great Armada had foundered.)

What an insight into her life is conveyed by her stark words: "My people had little property: all the land they possessed was the grass of two cows" or in that terrifyingly simple comment, "I had a pair of brothers who

3

lived." With no awareness of literature—at least as something so distinct from everyday living as to require schooling—she reflected the rich metaphor of a life lived far from abstractions: "He wouldn't travel as much as a cock's step from the house. . . ." "[Your mother] . . . thinks that it's out of your poll that the sun rises."

Life on the continental shelf of Europe—and that on an island with a primitive economy—might seem unimaginably remote from the stresses of modern urban life, but Peig recounts violence barely averted when Irish farmers faced English bayonets; the evictions of penniless families; roguery in the community; hunger in the home; the solitary pain of a child forced into domestic slavery. But what is inescapable in the retelling is the guiding ethos of the community—a combination of stoic acceptance ("'Fate exists, child,' my mother answered") and a religious joy in life ("The High King of Creation be praised and thanked . . . who ordained a livelihood for every creature according to nature!").

The islanders, however, lived in no romantic mist. The gentle irony of a marriage did not go unobserved: "I thought that the world was queer, to tie a fine boy like him to a tawny lump like her—but then indeed three hundred pounds [at least $6,000 by today's standards] gave her a fine complexion!"

But "dead indeed is the heart from which the balmy air of the sea cannot banish sorrow and grief." Resilience and buoyancy were the more common characteristics of Peig and the island community. Partly it derived from a highly developed sense of tradition: the great Irish tales of a thousand and more years ago never found a jaded audience during a drinking bout or at the nightly circling of the fireside, and phrases and allusions from these tales suffused the common speech. Even the baby in the house was dandled to the remembrance of tradition:

4

Muirisín's your name and Muirisín's your uncle
And Muirisín you've been to the seventh generation.

Partly the underlying optimism came from a firm belief in the nearness of God:

> I remember well when I was trying to work while at the same time the heart in my breast was broken by sorrow, that I'd turn my thoughts on Mary and on the Lord, and on the life of hardship *they* endured. I knew that it was my duty to imitate them and to bear my cross in patience. Often I'd take my little canvas sheet and face for the hill for a small amount of turf and on the road home the weight on my heart would have lifted. God's Son and His Glorious Mother are true friends!

And always the natural joy of unsophisticated life quickened the pulse. Work, food, sports, contest and exhibition, song, dance, and storytelling provided a depth of satisfaction which the same activities fail to provide in more sophisticated societies. "The old world will have vanished" (after her death) she tells us in awareness of the social, emotional, and psychological perimeters of her life on the Great Blasket Island. As layered, direct, and simple as the life it portrays, Bryan MacMahon's translation from Peig's native Irish is an appropriate tribute to that great-souled woman and her people. It may be that they were made of sterner stuff than we; it may be, too, that the life stories of Peig in Ireland and of Henry Conklin in upper New York State and of others elsewhere have yet something to offer us in the way of meeting our individual destinies.

St. Paul, Minnesota   Eoin McKiernan, *President*
Summer 1974   Irish American Cultural Institute

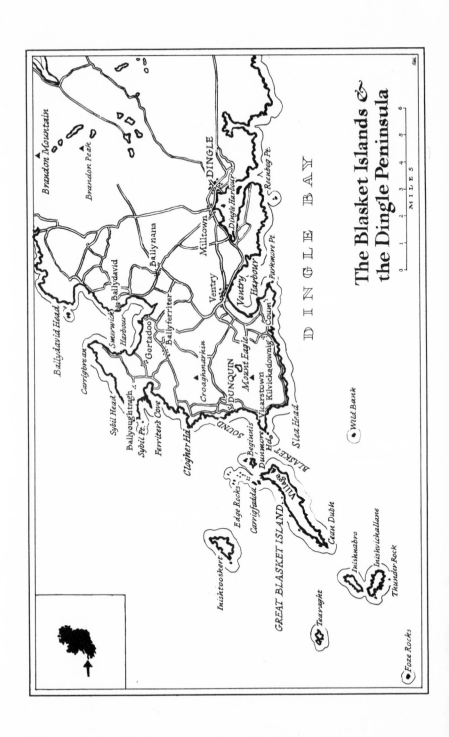

The Blasket Islands &
the Dingle Peninsula

MILES

0   1   2   3   4   5   6

DINGLE BAY

Brandon Mountain

Brandon Peak

DINGLE

Milltown

Ballynana

Ballydavid Head

Ballydavid

Smerwick
Harbour

Gortadoo

Ballyferriter

Carrigbrean

Sybil Head

Ballyoughteragh

Sybil Pt.

Ferriter's Cove

Clogher Hd.

Croaghmarhin

Ventry

DUNQUIN

Mount Eagle

Vicarstown
Kilvickadownig

Ventry
Harbour

Dingle Harbour

Reenbeg Pt.

Parkmore Pt.

Coum

SOUND

Beginnis

Dunmore
Hd.

Sleea Head

BLASKET

Wild Bank

Inishtooskert

Edge Rocks

Carrigfadda

GREAT BLASKET ISLAND

VILLAGE

Ceann Dubh

Tearaght

Inishnabro

Inishvickallane

Thunder Rock

Foze Rocks

TRANSLATOR'S NOTE

No praise of mine is needed to acknowledge the great debt due to Máire Ní Chinnéide, M.A., who persuaded Peig to tell her tale and who, with knowledge and fidelity, edited the text after it had been originally written down by Mícheál Ó Guithín, Peig's poet-son. In the course of her narrative Peig herself pays tribute to Máire in full measure.

I would like to call attention to something Máire noted in her preface to the original edition—the old custom that obtained on the Island by which a married woman was generally known by her maiden name, e.g. Peig Sayers for Peig Guiheen (Mrs. Peats Guiheen) and Cáit O'Brien for Cáit O'Connor (Mrs. Eoghan O'Connor).

So as to convey the tone and spirit of the original of this simple but moving autobiography I have tried in this translation to imagine how Peig Sayers would have told her story, had she been born on a small holding on the same Dingle Peninsula, but say, twenty-five miles to the east of Dunquin, where she and her people, though English-speaking, would have been only one-generation removed from Irish as a vernacular.

I acknowledge with sincerest thanks the kindness of two old friends, Liam de Brún, M.A., and Seosamh Ó Dálaigh, O.S., both of whom gave me most valuable advice in this translation. Liam has made a life-long study of the dialect of Irish spoken in Corkaguiny and spends a great deal of his time there, while Seosamh, in addition to making valuable recordings in various parts of Ireland as official collector of folklore for *Coimisiún Béaloideasa Éireann*, returned again and again to his native Dunquin officially to record the lore of his friend and neighbour Peig Sayers. He is also a son of the teacher-writer Seán Ó Dálaigh who figures in the text.

Buíochas óm chroí go hiomlán.

BRYAN MACMAHON.

An old woman sat up in bed in Dingle Hospital. Her hair was carefully combed.

As she sat in state, her sightless eyes vaguely alternating with her ears in sifting the occasions of the ward, a flock of schoolboys crowded to the stairhead and spilled quietly into the room.

As four boys walked forward, nuns and nurses watched carefully.

One of the four boys spoke in Irish. 'Peig Sayers,' he said, 'we offer you this small gift as a mark of our esteem . . .' *chun méid ár measa a chur in iúl duit . . .*

He thrust his gift into the blind woman's hands.

The tears came down the old features. Peig Sayers of the Blasket Island, one of the great narrators of the wonder-tales of Gaelic Ireland, and a superb natural actress, was on her deathbed.

In gratitude she stretched out her hands to read and caress the boy's face.

From HERE'S IRELAND by Bryan MacMahon.

EXPLANATORY FOREWORD TO THE
ORIGINAL EDITION

by

Mícheál Ó Guithín
(Poet-son of Peig Sayers)

Praise be to God! I little thought at one time in my life that such an important piece of literary work lay hidden in my mother's old grey head. I have no hesitation in saying, for what I say is true, that were it not for Máire Ní Chinnéide, my mother would have taken her tale with her into the grave. It was Máire who urged her to undertake the work: my mother argued fiercely that she couldn't do anything like that, until at long, long last she yielded. And so we began the task—she dictating the story and myself putting it down on paper.

Slow laborious work it was for the likes of us, for we had no exact knowledge of the business of literature. I understood well, dear reader, when I grasped my pen in my hand, that the best solution to my problem was to give my mother free rein and not to hinder her in the least in her telling.

And she drew the picture for me without a single flaw: a picture of a needy girl facing a harsh and difficult life— one which she neither knew nor understood. The story shows her on a hill-top on a warm day in summer—a barefooted girl thinking of her dear friend Cáit-Jim. And again she will be seen with a dirty coat-tail driving out the calves or leading them to water.

I admit that she told her story a great deal better than I had expected of her, for it is well known that at the time she told it she was a poor tormented old woman. However, thanks be to God, we now have the fruits of her labour. She thought (indeed she was certain of it!) that her life was in no way important and that nothing in it

9

was worth publishing, until Máire Ní Chinnéide and Léan Ní Chonalláin convinced her of the opposite. Now she's absolutely delighted that she consented to do as they had implored her!

She told me when first I started on the manuscript that all she could give me was guesswork and blind groping. As far as my opinion went, dear reader, I thought that laziness was at work in her, but the direct opposite was uppermost in her mind. Her spirits drooped because of the cloud of sorrow that stood as to the life before her mind's eye. But after a great deal of talk she moved freely through the tale.

The young people of Ireland should pray earnestly for the soul of this old woman when she is dead; they should also pray that Máire and her family may be lucky and happy, for after I had finished my work, *she* made a clear copy of the complete text. I did nothing but what I was bound to do—set down the story from my mother's lips to the best of my ability. This I wasn't loath to do—I'd do as much again for my mother's sake and for the sake of the Irish language.

Contents

The Days of My Youth

Myself as an infant — My people — My school dress —
My going to school — The Schoolmistress

I'M an old woman now, with one foot in the grave and the other on its edge. I have experienced much ease and much hardship from the day I was born until this very day. Had I known in advance half, or even one-third, of what the future had in store for me, my mind and heart wouldn't have been as gay or as courageous as they were in the beginning of my days.

The place in which I was born was a small remote townland in Dunquin at the foot of Mount Eagle—in the townland in which the legendary House of Mór stands. My father and mother didn't marry there; they did so in the parish of Ventry where they lived for some time before moving to Dunquin.

My people had little property: all the land they possessed was the grass of two cows. They hadn't much pleasure out of life: there was always some misfortune down on them that kept them low. I had a pair of brothers who lived—Seán and Pádraig; there was also my sister Máire.

As a result of never-ending flailing of misfortune my father and mother moved from the parish of Ventry to Dunquin; for them this proved to be a case of going from bad to worse, for they didn't prosper in Dunquin no more than they did in Ventry.

Tomás Sayers was my father's name and Peig Brosnan my mother's maiden name. She was a gentle, honest woman; in build she had once been broad-shouldered and strong. For the first six years after their marriage they prospered. They had three in family—two sons and a daughter: that was the sum total of the family that lived!

13

After that, one after another, the children died, until in all, nine children were buried. My poor mother was troubled and distracted as a result of the death of her children. Day after day her health and courage ebbed away until in the heel of the hunt the poor woman hadn't even the desire to live.

She got the idea firmly into her head that if she left the place where she was, maybe their luck would change. Thus she was forever nagging my father to be on the look-out for somewhere else instead of the place in which they then lived. By good fortune he heard that a man living in Vicarstown was selling his house and holding and that he intended emigrating to America. My father decided to buy the place and buy it he did; after the man in question and his family had gone off to America my father settled up his own land and my people then moved north from Ventry and took their place.

They were there only six months when I was born: my mother was delighted as I was growing up to her for I was the only one of the last ten children who lived: thus I was everyone's pet and especially the pet of my brother Seán. If even a puff of wind blew about my ears Seán would think that I'd lose the life! He wouldn't travel as much as a cock's step from our house without taking me along with him; even when he went 'cabin-hunting' in the evening he took me with him so that I'd have the other children of the neighbourhood as company.

On the eastern side of the little river there was only our house and the house of Muiris Scanlon. Four small thatched houses stood on the western side of the river: those of Seán Bán, Eoghan Brown, Séamas Boland and Seán Crohan. In each of those houses there was first-class company and in each one too, a small flock of children was growing to maturity. Those were the cross children! At that time Séamas Boland's was generally the 'rambling-house': the adults would be playing cards on the table and the youngsters would be in the corner carrying on children's games. Those of the children who were able to fend for themselves and who were attending school, had their books out learning their lessons for the following day.

14

I had, as they say, 'a great turn' for books and also 'a great mind' for the beautiful pictures they contained. Séamas had a dear little daughter—Cáit-Jim we called her—and she was very attached to me. She'd show me the pictures and she'd also tell me that she'd take me to school and that I'd have lovely little books similar to those she was showing me.

I'd be delighted if I had a small book of my own—one in which I could look at the pictures any time I liked. I had a great desire to go home that night and tell my mother that I intended going to school the next day.

So, I kept gabbing away to my brother Seán, asking him to take me home at once: he was slow enough to leave the cards behind him, but as I have already said, he was very fond of me.

'Wisha, I pity you, you poor little thing,' he said, 'I daresay you're sleepy.' He took me up in his arms.

Bedtime was then drawing near. At home, I washed my feet and took my seat on the little súgán stool by the fireside. When my mother had finished her prayers, I nuzzled my head artfully against her bosom. The poor woman put her arm around me and pressed me lovingly to her breast.

'Do you know that I'm off to school on Monday?' I said.

'School, is it?' she said with a laugh.

'Yes, indeed, a-girl! I'm off to school with Cáit-Jim.'

'Wisha,' said she, 'not saying I don't believe you, but isn't it early you have the mind for schooling? Aren't you too young yet to go to school?'

I was only four years of age at that time. My father spoke up and said: 'Let her have her own way! The school is no distance from her and she'll be better off there than breaking her bones jumping from fence to fence out here.'

'Better off indeed!' I said in reply, 'and I'll also have lovely little books!'

'God direct you to do what's right, child,' said my father and off we went to bed.

When I woke in the morning my father had just come in from the garden.

'Asleep yet, little woman?' he asked.

'I am, indeed,' I said, as I raised my head.

''Pon my word but it's fine for you,' he said, 'if that's the way you're preparing for going to school.'

I got out of bed and my sister Máire put on my clothes. When she had me well buttoned up we sat down to eat the morning meal. As we were eating, I spoke to Máire.

'Máire, girl,' I said, 'you'll have to make new clothes for me. I don't like going to school wearing a torn dress.'

'God knows,' Máire said, 'I've plenty to bother me besides sitting down now to sew.'

'Never mind that,' said my father, 'you won't be long stitching them between now and the time she goes.'

Máire was quite a grown-up girl at this time: she had to carry the burden of the house because my mother was of little use—she had lost her health and wasn't able to do a hand's turn. Thus, Máire had little time for making clothes for me, yet she liked me a great deal and didn't want to deny me my own way. As soon as she got the opportunity she started to make my dress and when that was finished she made a bib for me. When all the clothes were finished she said, 'My word, but you'll be the right little ball of a girl when you're wearing these!'

My heart was pounding with joy.

'You won't wear them now, pet, until the day you're going to school?'

'God bless us, Máire,' I said, 'what will my mother say when she sees them?'

'She'll be as proud as a peacock!' Máire said, 'for the dear woman thinks that it's out of your poll the sun rises!'

'Small blame to her for that,' replied my father. 'It's an ease to the poor woman's mind through all her troubles to see this child growing up to her after all her clutch that died!'

Well, Monday arrived and I was in great form because I was going to school. I looked back along the road and spied Cáit-Jim making for the schoolhouse as fast as her legs could carry her. When she saw me: 'Well, well, Peig,' says she, 'are you off to school today?'

17

'I am, Cáitín,' I said.

I went in home. Máire got my new clothes and put them on me. She washed my hands and face and tidied back my hair. When she was satisfied with me: 'My word!' she said, 'I've rigged you out as swanky as the daughter of any gentleman.'

I went up to the bed where my mother was lying.

'Look at me now, Mom-girl,' I said.

She laughed and said, 'Thanks be to the great God who spared you to me!'

'I'm going to school now, girl,' I told her. 'Cáit-Jim is waiting for me.'

Again she spoke up from the bed. 'Cáit, darling,' she said, 'when you're let out at midday, bring her home for a bite of food for she's too young and she'd be too long fasting.'

'I will,' said Cáit.

'The blessing of God go with you, child,' said my mother, and the pair of us girls went buck-jumping down the road.

When we reached the schoolhouse all the scholars had gathered there before us but the schoolmaster had not yet arrived. Before very long we saw him coming back along the road. There was a fine high wall outside the schoolhouse with three or four steps of a stile in it. When the Master reached this point the children ceased whatever clatter or noise they were making and became quiet. I was eyeing him and sizing him up closely.

He was a broad, low-sized, middle-aged chunk of a man and his appearance wasn't very healthy. He found it hard going to mount the steps but at last he succeeded in doing so. Reaching the doorway he drew a key out of his pocket and opened the door.

All the children trooped in and each class sat on its own bench. I held on to Cáit-Jim's hand with the grip of a drowning man and my two eyes were as big as bowls with fear and wonder. As great as was my delight in the morning, I promise you that I was mute enough now. My eyes darted here and there taking in every single detail. Then I heard the door opening. I looked towards it—a young-looking, slender, tall, dark slip of a woman was coming in.

She had an umbrella in her hand and a pair of yellow earrings on her ears. She never cried halt until she landed up to the table where the schoolmaster was sitting.

'God protect us, Cáit,' I said. 'Who would she be?'

'She's the schoolmistress, girl.'

'Would that be Julia?'

'The very woman!' said Cáit.

'Devil a lie but Poet Dunlea was right when he made that verse about her!'

'I don't know the verse. Do you?'

'As if so much would escape me!'

'Say it!' said Cáit. 'No one will hear us.'

'I'll say it so,' I said.

I began then:

> *He who would view this filly-foal, strolling beneath her parasol;*
> *Beads of gold in her ear-lobes, ringing like the bells of Rome;*
> *Saffron silks on her shoulders, her cheeks like the bloom of roses;*
> *Fairer than Niamh the Comely at the death of Talc Mac Trone.*

Young as I was at that time I had verses like that on the tip of my tongue, this because I was always listening to adults reciting. I was pert too and they had a habit of making me recite the verses for entertainment.

''Pon my soul,' said Cáit, 'the poet gave her a name she never earned. Isn't that one as slim and as black as an eel!' Then: 'Be quiet now,' she said, 'the rolls are being called.'

The schoolmaster started calling out the names in a loud voice and according as he called a name he'd be answered with 'Present, sir!' This done he called the Second Class up to the table: this was the class in which Cáit-Jim was enrolled.

19

'I don't know what I'll do with you now,' she told me.

'I'll go with you,' I said, at the same time keeping a firm grip on her. 'Twas no good for her to be at me; right up to the table I followed her and my head hanging with shame.

'By the holy!' said the Master. 'We have an extra scholar today.'

He came over to me and caught me by the hand. 'Who's your father, little girl?' he asked.

'Tom Sayers, Master,' I said.

'And what name have they on you?'

'Peig Sayers, Master,' I said again.

'I have it now,' he said and then he entered my name in the roll-book. He turned round and presented me with a little book with a red cover.

'Sit in there on that bench until Cáit-Jim goes back to you,' he said.

I was as delighted as if I had been presented with a cow.

I kept looking at my little book until the clock struck twelve. Then the door opened and the scholars raced out.

'Come along,' said Cáit-Jim, 'we won't be ten minutes going and coming.'

Off we scampered running at our best and when we reached Vicarstown, Cáit made off west to her own house. When I arrived home my mother was seated in the corner. She hugged me tightly: 'How did your day go, little one?' she asked. 'And how do you like going to school?'

'I like it very much, Mom,' I said. 'The Master is a very nice man. Look at the beautiful book he gave me.'

'It's no wonder he'd be nice to you, child,' she said, 'since he's a near relative of your own.'

'I won't be a bit afraid of him so!'

'No need for you to be afraid of him, girl. Dónal wouldn't harm anyone.'

'Is that his name, Mom?' I asked.

'Dónal Moriarty is his name but we call him Dónal-the-Master.'

She had a cup of milk boiled for me. She also had a piece of bread and I wasn't long munching that! I was just ready when Cáit-Jim came calling for me. Off we went hopping and jumping down the road. We needed to hurry as the Master was calling in the schoolchildren.

'I'd say,' said Cáit as we were making our way back to the schoolhouse, 'that you won't be allowed stay beside me now. The Mistress will put you in the Babies' Class.'

She was right, for when we went in, the schoolmistress put me sitting on the bench farthest from the front. There were about twenty children of my own age on the same bench.

'You'll be in this class from this out,' she told me.

I sat in shyly. There wasn't a murmur out of me, but I was watching everything. After a time the girl next to me spoke.

'Where are you from?' she asked.

'From Vicarstown,' I said.

'What's your name?'

'Peig Sayers.'

'God bless us! I'm from the Coum, and my name is Siobhán McCarthy.'

'And is the school far from you?'

''Tis indeed, a good bit.'

'Are you long at school?'

'I amn't then; only three weeks. I was terrified out of my wits in the beginning, but now it doesn't bother me at all.' Then she said: 'I'll be your friend. I have English and I'll tell you what the schoolmissus is saying.'

When I heard her saying this, I was satisfied. I was easy in my mind for the rest of the day peeping here and there and taking in everything. After a while I noticed two of the scholars who were grown up and who had nothing else to do but move here and there around the schoolroom. They were over sixteen years of age and I was greatly surprised that they were attending school considering how grown up they were.

As soon as the clock struck three the schoolmistress left us off home: Cáit-Jim caught me by the hand.

'Home we go, girl!' she said.

From that day forward I knew my way well.

21

When night fell, I was sitting at the fireside with a fine glowing fire in front of me and a pot of potatoes boiling on top of it. As he usually did, my father sat on the chair beside me. I questioned him.

'Dad,' said I, 'do you know those two big boys who are still going to school?'

'I do, child,' he said. 'Seán Daly and Tom, the Master's son are the boys you're referring to. Tomás is a son of the Master and Seán is his sister's son. Seán is an orphan; the Master thinks a great deal of him. People say that he'll get the school when the Master dies because the Master's own son is a pure *gligín* and he can get no good of him at all. They say he'd rather be off to America than stick to the school."

'Well, then,' I said, answering him, 'I'd prefer the Master we have because he's very quiet.'

'Indeed, child,' my father said. 'Things aren't always to our likes.'

By this time the potatoes were boiled.

Affairs of Home and School

Pádraig's return — How Seán got his nickname — A son's wife in the house — The death of the old schoolmaster — A new teacher

WHEN we had the potatoes eaten my father and Seán went off rambling to the neighbours' houses. There was no one with myself then except Máire who was knitting and it wasn't long until I fell asleep. When my father returned I was awake. I heard him say to my mother: 'Pádraig will be coming home on Saturday.'

'God welcome him!' my mother said.

My heart jumped for joy for they were referring to my brother Pádraig. It was now more than a year since last he was at home and he had been in service since he was twelve years of age. Although I was far more attached to Seán because of his being so often around the house, just the same, I had a sincere welcome for Pádraig.

A couple of days went by and on Saturday evening Pádraig walked in the door. I ran to meet him; he took me up in his arms and kissed me lovingly. Then he put his hand into his pocket and handed me a huge paper bag of sweets. Along comes Máire to relieve me of some of them! I gave her some and I also gave a share to my mother. Then I began chewing away as best I could.

Pádraig was telling of the exciting events of the year; then he said to my father, 'I'm finished with Killarney!'

'Why so?' my father asked.

'I couldn't live there with the loneliness. I liked the mistress very much but now that she's dead I'll never again cross the top of John Street in Dingle on my way to the east.'

'Fair enough, sonny,' said my father. ''Tis as well for you to be doing something for yourself,' and off he went for the cows.

By this time my brother Seán had grown to marriageable age. Máire was a grown girl too and it was about time for her to settle down. She couldn't leave the house until some woman had come in to carry on the business of the place. My mother was very low in spirits and couldn't do a single thing: for this reason Seán would have to marry.

Not like nowadays, it was easy for a young man to get a wife at that time for very few people were emigrating to America and this left young women plentiful.

At the time I'm referring to, my brother Seán was one of the most powerful and finest young men in Kerry. There was no limit to his strength: because he was so strong he had earned the nickname of 'The Pounder'.

It was a Sunday afternoon and the young men of the parish had gathered at the cross-roads. They were testing one another to see who best could raise a great heavy stone off the ground. Some of them succeeded in doing so.

'The dickens sweep you, Seán,' said Gabha Beag— the little blacksmith—'is there any stuff in you at all?'

Seán raised another huge stone and placed it down on top of the first one. Then he got his hands under the two stones together and lifted them without the slightest bother. That was something that no one else could do. Gabha Beag ran over to him and caught him by the hand.

'More power to your arm, Seán,' he said. 'No doubt in life about it but you're better than 'Pounder' Kennedy the best day ever he stood in the prime of his manhood!'

All the people gave a great roar of applause. That nickname followed Seán Sayers until this very day, for ever after he was never called anything but 'The Pounder.' But that same didn't lessen the good opinion everyone had of him.

The following year he married a girl from the parish of Ventry—her name was Cáit Boland. I was seven years of age at that time.

The following year my brother Pádraig married a daughter of Seán Bán from our own townland. She was a gentle girl but she was also wise and intelligent: we used call her Máire Sheáin Bháin.

A short time afterwards my sister Máire married a Kennedy man from the parish of Ventry. Every one of them now was doing for himself or herself but I was still a charge on my father and he had his hands full for he was a hard-working labouring man.

From the day my brother Seán married, I think my father knew little peace of mind for his daughter-in-law Cáit was fiery-tempered and apt to flare up on occasions. If he lobbed that hill over there down on top of this hill here in order to please her she wouldn't be thankful to him in the evening.

My father, however, was a quiet, sensible man with no mind whatsoever for trouble or wrangling and because of this he often turned a deaf ear to his daugher-in-law when she was in a tantrum. I often listened to them and I had pity for my father when I heard the tongue-lashing she gave him. What I've come to understand now and I think it true, is that it was for my sake and for the sake of my mother who hadn't her health that he put up with so much of this lacerating. It often seemed that if he had a heart of stone he'd have to make her some back-answer — but he never did! The only answer he ever gave her was:

'Indeed, you'd be better off with a bit of sense, my girl.'

But where's the use in talking? Doesn't the old proverb say 'Advising a rough-spoken woman is as senseless as striking cold iron with a rib of hair.'

By this time I was getting quite precocious and I had to do many little jobs about the house. I had also to herd the cattle whenever my father and my brother, Seán, were busy.

I was attending school every day and I was getting on well. I missed my lessons very rarely because we were at them hard and fast when we came together at night. We had the habit of coming together in Jim's house. Jim was a pleasant man on his own floor and a good scholar into the bargain. Thus, every word we couldn't understand and every problem we couldn't unravel he'd solve them for us and he'd make us understand what they were all about.

He had four daughters of his own and two sons—a handy clutch—although only one of them outlived him— and that was Cáit-Jim. One after another they died when they were grown men and women—God save the hearers!

One fine day in the month of June, Cáit-Jim and myself had gone off very early to school. We had no idea whatsoever what time of day it was, except to make a guess at it, because at the time I'm referring to not one of us had a clock in the house! Because of this we were a long time waiting at the school before anyone else arrived to join us. But, after a while, the other scholars began to gather and we were then waiting for the Master who had not as yet arrived. After half an hour or so we saw him coming along the road from the east; he was walking slowly and his face was very pale.

'God save us, Cáit-girl,' I said, 'doesn't the Master look very white today?'

'He does, indeed,' she said. 'I daresay he's not very well.'

By this time he was at the foot of the steps that led up to the schoolhouse. He placed his hand on the fence in order to steady himself as he went up. He was standing on the top step when the two legs were taken from under him and the poor man was flung right down on the point of his poll on the hard road.

All the children screeched and screamed; with the terrible hullabaloo we made, a man from Ballinglanna heard us. When he arrived on the spot where the Master was stretched out, the poor teacher was only barely alive. The man sent two of the schoolboys to look for help. A crowd of people arrived on the scene, a messenger went off for the priest and the others carried the Master to his own house.

The priest came and anointed him. Father Liam Egan was the Parish Priest at that particular time. The last word Dónal-the-Master said to him was:

'Father! Look after my sister's son and give *him* the school since my own son didn't stay to mind it.'

'Very well, Dónal,' said the priest. 'The blessing of God on you now.'

Dónal didn't live long after this and Master Daly got the school when he died. He got a long life in charge of it—and may God grant a long life to his son in charge of the school after him again. There's no doubt whatsoever but that Master Daly was a good man, a clever teacher and a great warrant to solve every problem.

We had the new Master now and indeed if we had, he was a good deal more intimidating than old Dónal! He was quick and lively and young and courageous—and cross enough he was too when he failed to get anything that was right or proper into our skulls! Honest, it was often I got a clatter of the palm of the hand from him that made me see visions galore!

I remember clearly the first time that Irish came into the schools. Our own school was one of the first in Kerry in which Irish was taught and it wasn't too hard to teach it to the children of Dunquin since it was in that language, as they say, we were bred, born and reared. And we had an intelligent and learned schoolmaster to teach it to us —the rough road and the smooth!

I remember well when I first began to learn Irish: my little schoolbook had Irish on one side of the page and the English translation on the other. I think it was '*Bó bhán,* a white cow,' '*Gamhain breac,* a speckled calf,' and words like that, that were printed in the book. But that small amount was all the while increasing and whatever was missing from the text the teacher could supply it very well indeed. I had no fault whatsoever to find with him! Even though I'm an old woman now I am very proud to have it to say that Seán Daly was my school-teacher.

Shortly afterwards it was rumoured that the Master and the Mistress were going to Dublin to take out some certificates in Education. This proved to be true for on the following Friday evening when he was about to let us home:

'I'm leaving you for a while,' the Master told us, 'and I won't be back here for nine months. Whatever cause of complaint you've had about my crossness I promise you that the little boyo who's invoiced will be far worse. He's the man who'll knock smoke out of ye!'

Man alive, he frightened the living life out of us and we had no topic of conversation from that until the following Monday but the evil and bad-tempered schoolmaster who was coming to us. 'But what is thought is never wrought!'

On Monday morning when we arrived at school, neither Cáit-Jim nor myself cast a thought on the lessons;

our minds were taken up with the kind of schoolmaster we'd find before us.

'Gracious, Cáit, I don't know in the world if he'll be kind to us?'

'For heaven's sake, girl,' said Cáit, 'he won't! I daresay that no one is ever like one of your own.'

We were like this discussing our affairs until we walked right into the schoolhouse. Some of the scholars were before us and others were coming along behind. Each one went up and sat on his own bench since we had no permission to talk now. I looked up in the direction of the table.

A strange man was standing there; he had a yellowish complexion and black curly hair. He was thick-set, plump and strong and indeed he showed the sign of the feeding he had got as an infant!

'God save us—it's the new Master,' I said in my own mind.

A young woman was sitting on a chair beside him. She had black hair and her skin was as white as snow. Her complexion was a mixture of red and white and she had two lively merry eyes in her head. She wasn't tall but she was nicely made and well-proportioned. The single flaw I could find on her was the pock-marks that had deeply pitted her features. 'You're the new mistress,' I told myself and that she certainly was—and a kind, quiet teacher too.

After a while she got up off the chair and the Master sat down in her place. He began to call out the names and, man dear, we were amazed, for if we didn't know that it was rolls he was calling we wouldn't have understood him! He had such a foreign accent on his speech that he could have been a big bucko of an Englishman over from the city of London! He hadn't one tittle of Irish in his beak! But if he hadn't itself, he was well able to teach the scholars. I well remember that when we were sitting on the benches writing in our copy-books or doing our Arithmetic he had a habit of stealing up behind us and listening very carefully—that was because we'd generally be spouting Irish to one another when we got the chance. On account of this he'd be paying great attention and trying to pick up every single word. But, oh dear, he had a right job on hands, for he had to spend a long time at it so as to soften that awful cramp he had in his tongue!

He gave nine months teaching us and I have to admit that he never touched a child in the school with a stick or with his open palm during that time. When he had cause for complaint about any pupil he'd catch a rib of his hair and give it a tug. He was a fine, quiet, sensible young man and everyone in the parish had great affection for him: James Gleeson was his name and he came from Castle-island.

The very day before he left for home was his last day in school. He gave sweets to every child, big and small, and then he said goodbye and asked God to bless every one of them.

The following Monday our own Master and Mistress returned: we were delighted and overjoyed especially since they had come out on top in the examinations!

I am a Cause of Strife

An unfought battle — A sweet cake — Desire is powerful! —
My father and his son's wife—Mention of putting me in
service

AT that time the Land Question was causing the country
great concern and the landlords were inclined to threaten
the tenants. They had to get their rent or their land! If the
rent wasn't forthcoming the tenant would be pitched out
without mercy. Here and there the people were up in arms
against them but the landlords and their followers were
too powerful. Alas! it's many the poor widow and orphan
they flung out on the side of the road without pity, mercy
or compassion.

Rumour had it at that time that Muiris Ferriter of
Ballyoughtragh was to be thrown out of his land the
following week. Now was the time for the people of
Corkaguiny to stand up for their rights! Tomás Martin of
Gortadoo was the leader of the Land League and whatever
he would say was obeyed by all the boys. So they were
well advised by him as to what was the best course of
action to be taken on the day of trial.

I don't think there ever was as much uproar and hullabaloo in the parish of Ballyferriter as there was on the day
fixed by the bailiffs to take possession of Ferriter's place.
Every man, young and old, able to carry a weapon of any
kind had headed for the gathering place appointed by
Captain Martin.

I remember well, that about noon on that day, the
Master closed the schoolhouse door and those of us who
were able to look after ourselves went with him east to
Ardroe from where we had a good view of the crowds.

Although we were not close to the people and didn't
know how they were setting to work there was a tremen-

dous spectacle to be seen—hundreds of men, young and old, each with his own weapon on his shoulder. Those who hadn't pikes had furze grubbers, staves and other weapons that could really cause havoc.

I heard people say afterwards that were it not for the Parish Priest who made some compromise between them it is unknown what would have happened for when the crown forces—the peelers, the sheriff and the bailiffs— came on the scene, someone fired a missile at them. No sooner had this happened than their captain gave an order to his men that boded trouble!

And if he did, Captain Martin also gave an order to *his* men. 'Fix bayonets!' said the English captain. 'Fix pikes, boys!' said the Irish captain. Immediately hundreds of pikes and cudgels were raised aloft; however, the Parish Priest arrived and soon made a settlement.

To the best of my belief the English wouldn't have reached home in safety because some of Martin's men had dug deep trenches across the roads but, my sorrow and woe, those who'd accept a bribe were always with us and always will be, and someone who played the spy and got a lump sum of money for doing so, advised the English not to return by the road by which they had come, but to take a different route as the roads were trenched before them.

The police gave no indication of what they had in mind and they went home by a different road. It was a good job for them that they did so because the plan the Irish had decided on was this: when they'd find the English hemmed in on the roadway they'd move up behind them and more than likely there would have been a dreadful grapple. Just as well the story turned out as it did for no one was wounded nor lost his life!

When we arrived home that evening the sole topic of conversation was the hullabaloo in Ballyferriter that day. When I myself reached home, at any rate, I was as hungry as a ploughman. Potatoes out of the embers, roasted fine and hot—that was my fare. My mother gave me a lump of butter and a drop of new milk and I assure you that I had no fault whatsoever to find with my food. No one, young or old, had white bread or tea at that time.

I had barely finished the meal when Cáit-Jim arrived. Then it was noise and chatter about the bailiffs and the police! My father was sitting on a chair beside us filling his pipe with tobacco. 'Bad cess to ye!' he said, 'if ye haven't the foolish chatter!'

We drew in our horns quickly; after a while Cáit-Jim asked me; 'Have you the price of your schoolbook for tomorrow?'

'No! Unless I get it from my father.'

'Cat and skin go together, child!' said my father. 'Does the book cost much?'

'Thruppence,' I said.

'The Almighty spare us! 'Tis a poor pocket that'd miss it. But whisper! Take half-a-dozen eggs back the road to Ould Kitty and she'll give you the thruppence.'

'That's just the point,' I said, 'if I get the eggs.'

'You will! Why wouldn't you get them?'

I didn't trust my sister-in-law very far, but I'd have plenty time to ask her for the eggs in the morning. My father had no security in the house, you understand. Cáit-Jim went off to learn her lessons and I spent the rest of the evening by the fire listening to my father and Old Muiris telling stories until it was time to go to bed.

When I got up in the morning the question of the price of the schoolbook was going round and round in my head and I didn't know in the name of high heaven how I would ask for the eggs. But the morning was slipping away and the children of the neighbourhood were ready for school. At last my patience was exhausted.

'Cáit, dear, would you give me six eggs?' I said coaxingly to my sister-in-law.

'What do you want them for?'

'I want a schoolbook and it costs thruppence. I'll give the eggs to Ould Kitty and I'll get the pennies from her.'

She gave me the eggs and then I felt as rich as rich could be. Back across the stream I went; Ould Kitty was in her cabin before me, squatting on her hunkers and the

33

little hovel black with smoke around her. I gave her the eggs and asked for the threepence. She rose to her feet and went to a little cupboard in the lower part of the house.

She set the eggs aside and pulled out a long roomy purse that had several small pockets in it. The pence were in one pocket, the shillings in another and the little sixpenny bits in a third.

While she was groping for the pennies—this because if a finger was poked into your eye you wouldn't see it with the smoke—I spied a loaf of bread inside on a shelf on the cupboard. It was a cake made of snow-white flour with apple filling in the middle and sugar on the top. I was taken by an unmerciful desire to taste the cake and straight-away the temptation struck me to snatch some of it. I had very little time to do much thievery; what I had to do, I did in a hurry. I dug my talons into the cake—Ould Kitty was squatting below me—made two halves of it and rammed one of the halves right under my oxter.

Ould Kitty handed me the pennies.

'Is it going to school you are now, my pet?' she asked.

''Tis indeed,' I said and off I legged it out the door. I assure you that she wouldn't have been so sweet-tongued if she had known that Peig had stolen the sweet cake!

Cáit-Jim was waiting for me at the end of the boreen.

'The others are gone off long ago,' she said.

'Don't bother about them! That's all the better,' said I, and when we got out of sight of the houses I took my chunk of cake out from under my armpit.

'Look, Cáit dear, what I have!'

'Lord above in Heaven! Where did you get that?' Cáit asked.

'Stole it from Ould Kitty, girl,' said I.

To see a piece of white bread at that time was something of a marvel. But *we* had it now—a fine long piece of flour loaf, as sweet as honey, made of apples, sugar and other ingredients.

'Hurrah!' said Cáit. 'We'll have one gala day!'

'Whisper, Cáit, what will I do if Ould Kitty finds out that it was I stole her sweet loaf?'

'She'll never find out! How will she find it out? Sure she wasn't watching you!'

34

'She wasn't,' I said with a kind of remorse beginning to come over me just the same, 'but there was Someone looking at me and I'd prefer now not to have touched it. This was the very first roguery that entered my head and look how I gave into it. God save my soul, Ould Kitty will be all out cursing me and my father will be far worse to me if he comes to hear of it.'

'Cut the Sign of the Cross on yourself,' said Cáit-Jim, 'and ask God to protect you from her.'

'Oho,' said I, 'isn't it fine and easy you have the cure?'

By this time we were at the schoolhouse door.

'Lord above!' I said to Cáit, 'the Rolls are being called. Will we go in?'

'It'll only be a few wallops,' Cáit said, 'and we won't feel them as our stomachs are full.'

In we went and if we did, the Master glared angrily at us.

'Up here to the table!' he ordered.

Marching straight ahead we went right up; I was nearest to him. 'Out with your hand!' he said.

I stretched out my hand class of lazily and I got a whack and two whacks and so on until I got four in all. Poor Cáit-Jim got the same ration; we turned away from the table and sat into our benches.

It's a wonder that Ould Kitty wasn't turned into burned embers that day after we had gone home as a result of all the curses she got from us!

I bought the book I needed and I remember well that it was the first story in Irish I read; I hadn't the slightest remembrance of the trouncing I got from the Master for I had my wee new book going home.

That evening as I was making for my own door after returning from school I heard the ding-dong and tally-ho going on inside.

'Fine!' I told myself, 'That's Ould Kitty complaining me and the fat is rightly in the fire now!'

I felt really down and out and 'twas against my will I faced for the door. But she wasn't inside at all but some of the old barging was going on, for as I was going in I heard my father say:

'A woman is more stubborn than a pig! And a pig is more stubborn than the devil!' He was addressing his daughter-in-law.

'What's wrong with ye?' I asked.

'Never mind, child,' he told me. 'Eat your bit of food as long as you get it.' He left me then, his pipe alight, and he didn't return to the house until nightfall.

Not a sound out of anyone in the household for the rest of the evening!

Old Muiris had a habit of coming 'cabin-hunting' to our place every night.

'Isn't Muiris taking a long time to come tonight?' I said, and with that Muiris came in the door. He sat down on a chair by the fireside and my father and himself began threshing out the affairs of the world.

There was no outsider but Muiris in our house at that time. Seán and his wife had crossed over to the other side of the stream. My mother was asleep in the corner. I was sitting on a little stool by the hearth with my new book in my hand but instead of paying attention to the book I was listening far more keenly to my father telling his troubles to Muiris.

'And what have you to do?' Muiris asked.

'What I've made up my mind to do,' said my father, 'if I got any suitable place, I'd put that unfortunate girl there in service.'

'You would?'

'What else could I do?' my father replied. 'I'm convinced that if she were out of the house I'd have more peace of mind than I have. They consider the old woman in the corner no small charge on them besides carrying the expense of the girl too. She'll have food and clothing whatever way the wind blows and she won't cause anyone dissatisfaction.'

When I heard this I started crying.

'Stop that!' my father said. 'The matter doesn't concern you for the present. Don't mention a single word of this to anyone!'

'I won't,' I said and lowered my head.

They drew down some other topic of conversation for the rest of the night. It was close to bedtime then.

'Here's good night to ye,' said Old Muiris.

'Good luck go with you,' said my father.

As soon as he had gone away each one went on his knees and said a prayer. I went to bed, but if I did, I couldn't get a wink of sleep for I was going over and over what my father had said to Muiris. What would I do when I'd leave my own home? Where would I go? And who would be there to do a hand's turn for my mother? As I've said before, her health was gone and who would give her a drink when she needed it? My father wouldn't be at home always and there would be no one to tell her a single item of news and to make matters worse she was getting a little hard of hearing. From that out she'd have neither consolation nor comfort for I was the only consolation she had. Now I'd be gone and I wouldn't be able to help her at all. Her son, Seán, indeed would surely be kind to her, but that didn't make much difference for when the cat is out the mice dance!

All those thoughts were running in and out through my mind in such a way that cold sweat broke out through me and at long last I fell asleep. When I awoke in the morning the sun was shining brightly. I got up out of bed and put on my clothes.

'God direct me!' I said to myself. 'I'll have plenty time to think things out. Nothing for it now but to put the thought of the evil day on the long finger.'

How I Heard Stories in My Young Days

Races' Day draws near—'Clear the road; Father Owen is coming!'—How a pair of us got the pennies—Father Owen and the parson

CÁIT, my brother's wife, was busy around the house. She had a griddle of firm yellow-meal bread baking on the fire.

'Are you ready?' she asked me. 'If you are, off with you and call them to their food.'

They weren't far from home: standing on top of the fence I called my father.

When they came in, Cáit put the bread and plenty of milk on the table before us. Everyone was eating heartily except my father. The poor man's teeth weren't good: he suffered from a perpetual toothache and because of his rotten teeth he was making no hand of the yellow-meal bread. A regular complaint of his was that he suffered most when the supply of potatoes was exhausted.

Before we had finished the meal I saw Cáit-Jim coming from the west and she had every hop-skip-and-jump on the roadway. In she comes in a tremendous hurry.

'Devil a lie, Peig,' she said, 'but I have news!'

'How well you must always have some story, Cáit!' said my father. 'What's the great news you have this time?'

'Races on Ventry Strand in a fortnight's time!'

'Here comes God's help!' my father said.

'Will you go there, Tom Sayers?' she asked.

'Damn full sure I will! I never yet let Races pass without attending them. And another thing, maybe I'll be growing grass when Races-time comes round again.'

'Will *you* go?' Cáit-Jim asked me.

'I will indeed, if I'm allowed,' I answered.

'Be certain you'll be allowed,' said my father. 'You have two firm little ankle bones that'll walk you there and back again.'

Man dear! when I heard that, my heart was quivering with joy.

'I'll go too,' said Cáit-Jim. 'We'll start putting our pennies together and maybe we'll end up with a shilling for sweets.'

'Maybe so, girl,' I said and off she went from me all agog with joy.

But I had little prospect of a shilling or even of a sixpenny-bit at that time. After a while my father came and put a red coal of fire on his pipe.

'I have to go to the hill,' he said, 'and as there's no one else to look after the cows, be a good girl and mind them down in Diarmuid's field and I'll let you go to the Races.'

The weather was very warm and a good part of the day had passed by the time the cows were let out. About two o'clock or so the heat began to slacken a great deal.

'Just as well for me to let out the cows to you!' said Cáit. 'Drive them west before you but watch yourself at the gap for fear a stone'd fall down on your feet.'

'Drive them off to the west,' I said, 'until I get my little bag of books.'

When she came in she gave me a cut of bread and butter: 'Be chewing that for fear you'ld be hungry,' she said.

I was chewing away for myself as I went down the road. The cows had stopped before me in the gap and I took the stones out of the way and let them in before me. I sat beside the fence in a spot where there was delightful warmth and took out a book containing little verses in English. One of these verses I had to have memorized for Monday, but since I had Saturday and Sunday long enough before me I had plenty of time for that. The poem in question was 'There came to the Beach a Poor Exile of Erin.' I was very interested in the poem with the result that it wasn't very long until I had it off by heart.

By this time the weather was nice and cool and the sun

was slipping westward over the ridge of the Coum. The clear blue air hung above my head and the small birds were flying merrily from bush to bush. A great yellow bumble-bee buzzed as she flew past my ear: she landed on a bush in bloom a short distance away from me. I was watching her as she moved busily from flower to flower and before long another bumble-bee followed the first one and she too was industrious! As I watched them they reminded me of the song that Old Muiris was singing a week before—this when he had a drop of drink on board—after coming back from Dingle. Here was the verse he had:

> *Glory to You, God the Father, in the Heavens high!*
> *Illustrious Your name, and illustrious Your sway;*
> *For the humble honey-bees, a living You supply,*
> *That the finest scholars wouldn't master in their*
> *day.*

I heard the children making a commotion near the bridge back the road and when I stood up to see what was happening I saw a horse and side-car approaching: there were four passengers on the vehicle—two young women, a boy and the driver. The youngsters had this merry yelp of: 'Clear the road, Father Owen is coming!' and they were clipping the heels of each other and bouncing off the highway. Down I went to where Cáit-Jim was herding her own cattle.

'Hey, Cáit-Jim,' I said, 'Look at the coachful of gentry coming! We'll wait here on the fence until it passes.'

By this time it was a little to our side of Frawley's Bridge and my! it was moving at a right pace! Quick as wink it was directly in front of us: it came to a halt and this huge tall man hopped down from it. He wasn't too old and somehow he had the glossy shine of money about him. He spoke to us in English and although we weren't too well able to answer him we understood what he was saying: he wished to see 'The House of Mór.' and he asked us if we could point it out to him. Cáit-Jim—for 'twas she answered him—said that she could, and then

40

he spoke to the two girls and they came off the side-car. Off with us up the road—Cáit-Jim and myself leading the way and the other three bringing up the rear.

When we reached the place where the House once stood the man was really surprised because he could see only the single grave. The girls began to examine the writing on the pointed stone that stood at the grave-head; they had a camera and they took pictures of the place. The man put Cáit and myself standing side by side and they took our photographs. Then they left the place and the two of us walked side by side with them until we reached the end of the road where the side-car was waiting. The man gave each of us a shilling and off they went. As soon as they were clean out of our sight there was never a hare on Mount Eagle ran as fast as the pair of us for our hearts were simply flying with joy.

'See now, girl,' said Cáit, 'what did the old proverb say but that the help of God was nearer than the door! Look, haven't we both enough money for Races Day?'

'True!' I said. 'We'll have plenty of apples and sweets and we'll be independent of everyone!'

'Not a mortal penny will anyone get!' said Cáit. 'Off you go now for I think the small cow has broken out of the field!'

I went up and it gave me all I could do to put the cow in because her belly was full and she was inclined to head for home. I remained there jumping out of my skin with delight until I got the call to turn the cows home.

That night when we had the supper eaten, Seán went off to join the card-players, and Cáit took her stocking and went over to Seán Bán's house for a bout of gossip. She told me to tidy the table and to sweep out the floor; I was only barely ready when Muiris and Jim walked in the door.

'Blessing o' God on ye!' Jim said.

'And on you likewise,' said my father. 'By hell, Jim, it's a cure for sore eyes to see you!'

'When the darkness falls I don't fancy poking about,' Jim replied.

They sat beside the fire and commenced talking about the affairs of the world as old people generally do when they are in one another's company.

'You were in Dingle yesterday, Jim,' said my father. 'Did you bring back any news?'

'Devil a news except the great races that will be held on Ventry Strand. You'll go?'

'I never let the Races pass yet,' said my father. 'It's only one day in a lifetime and we'll knock right value out of it.'

'Be sure!' said Jim. 'We'll all go! Ventry isn't so far away and if the day is fine we'll wet our whistles.' Each of them was wild out about the drop of drink.

I was sitting above in the corner listening to them.

'Be certain that myself and Cáit will go too, Jim,' said I.

'Ha-ha-ddy, you little prattler! What do *ye* want there for? Indeed, ye'd want a pocketful of pennies to go there!'

'We have pennies a-plenty,' I said with a class of a pout.
My father turned on me.

'Where would you get the pennies?' he asked rather
suspiciously.

'We got the full of our hands of money today from
gentry!'

'Where were they?' Jim asked.

'A side-car came east to Frawley's Bridge and the man
and two women in it wanted to see the House of Mór.
Cáit and myself were before them at the bottom of the
road and the man asked us to show him the place. When
they were leaving they gave us a shilling each. That's
where we got it, boy!' I said.

'Hm! If that's the way things are, ye have plenty money
for sweets.'

'We have, man!' I said with delight. 'All the small lads
from Ballinglanna were there shouting: "Clear the road!
Father Owen is coming!" Why were they saying that?
What was the meaning of it?'

'I don't know child,' Jim said, 'but I hear that class of
talk quite often in people's mouths. No one can explain
that better than your father.'

'Do *you* know, Dad?' I asked him.

'Indeed, I should, girl,' he said. 'If I had tobaccy in my
pipe I'd tell ye the great story of Father Owen.'

When he had enough smoked, he drew the chair in
towards the fire and settled himself for talk. I prodded
Muiris in the knee because he was dozing off to sleep.

'Shake yourself up, Muiris!' I said. 'My father is
going to tell a story.'

'Wisha, by Gor!' said Muiris. 'It comes best from him.
I *was* falling asleep.'

'You're poor company, Muiris,' Jim said.

'Right you are!' said Muiris. '*I* never told a story in
my life.'

'It's no wonder I'd know about Father Owen,' said my
father, beginning his tale. 'Indeed he was my Parish
Priest early in my days. And 'twas he married me.'

'He had a great reputation,' said Jim. 'for the fine
stand he made for the unfortunate tenants and the Cath-
olics at that time.'

'I don't think,' my father went on, 'that there was another priest in Kerry who made a better stand against the crooked laws and the persecution of the Faith than did Father Owen. He was a Canon in Dingle, and a religious and pious churchman too. He went very hard against the 'soupers' who were plentiful in the locality in those days. On account of that the Protestants were forever disparaging him and running him down. But in sure, it was little good for them to be reviling him because in those times everyone held Father Owen O'Sullivan in the highest affection and esteem. A good right they had to do so; often in the Courthouse he stood up for the poor and pleaded for their rights. Thus the "other crowd" would rather that a mouthful of water would drown him and for a long while they watched their chance to embarrass him'.

'At that time,' my father went on, 'the Mass-house stood in East Ventry, and the Protestant Church wasn't forty yards away from it. An immense throng of people attended the Protestant Church in those days although there's neither trace nor tidings of them there today, thanks a hundredfold to God!'

'Wisha!' said Jim answering him, 'to this day Father Owen's name and fame are still mentioned with respect by the people and there isn't trace nor tidings of the "other crowd" left in any part of the locality.'

'Right!' said my father. 'Although that wasn't how matters stood the day the parson tried to get the upper hand of the priest on the road as both of them were returning home after the Sunday service. Each had a horse and carriage; the parson was in the driver's seat before Father Owen and so he had the start of him. Father Owen was an active reckless young man and whenever he went riding on his saddle-horse you'd love to see the furious speed at which he travelled. He didn't like to have anything on the road before him—the way would have to be clear for him, and that's the reason, child,' he said to me, 'that that was a common catch-cry among the people, for as soon as ever he'd draw near, those who had English could be heard shouting at the tops of their

44

voices: "Clear the road! Father Owen is coming!"'

'Heavens!' I said, 'that's the explanation of what the lads were saying in the evening when they saw the speed of the side-car.'

'That's it for sure,' said Muiris putting in his piece. 'Carry on, Tomás,' he added then.

'The two horses were knocking sparks out of the road, the parson holding his place in front of the priest all the while until they swung around Milltown Bridge and moved towards the east. Neither uttered a syllable until then.

'Father Owen raised his voice: "Half the road, please!" he said, but the parson pretended not to hear him. The priest spoke a second time, but if he did, the parson paid him little heed. The priest flew into a rage and lashed his own horse with the whip so as to pass between the parson and the fence. But that boyo wasn't caught napping for he reined in his horse directly in front of the priest. "You won't do that a second time!" the priest said and he stuck him to the ground there in the middle of the road. "Stay there now!" the priest said cantering east past him.'

'And tell me this, Tom' said Muiris, 'what did the parson do then?'

'Remained there on the roadside, my boy, himself and his horse for two hours and more,' said my father. 'He was petrified in that spot and he was a pure laughing-stock before the whole world. But when Father Owen's temper cooled he realized that he'd be foolish to put his head in the halter of the law. He knew well that that other unfortunate breed only wanted a chance to come at him. When he and the other three priests with him had the dinner eaten, he gave a skit of a laugh. "What's making you laugh, Father Owen?" Father O'Connor asked. "This—I think I've made a mess of things," said Father Owen. "The parson has only now reached his own house." "What happened him?" Father O'Connor wanted to know and Father Owen told them the story. "But," he added, "I'm afraid my fun will turn to earnest now."'

'I daresay,' said Jim, 'that they only wanted half an excuse to down him.'

'That was all!' said my father. 'The upstarts were powerful everywhere at that time. When the rumour spread that Father Owen had made a laughing-stock of the parson, he was hauled before the law in quick time.'

'He was fined, I daresay?' I asked.

'Fined he was, child,' my father said, 'and well-fined too! But they weren't satisfied inasmuch as they failed to land him in jail for a stiff term. They didn't get that satisfaction, for on Court Day the people of Dingle had as much money collected as would pay the fine twice over. And the foreign bucks were thoroughly disgusted at their failure to land the priest in a hobble.'

'I'd say, Tomás,' said Muiris, 'that it was hard enough on the people of Dingle to put that great haul of money together since times then were hard on poor people.'

'What are you saying, man?' my father said. 'They'd pledge their immortal souls before they'd let their own enemies and the enemies of their religion have that much satisfaction! They made nothing at all of the amount of money they lost to him. Act fast, that was the only course open to them from the moment they could cut the rope nearest the throat!'

'Dead right!' Muiris said, 'I suppose that enough money was collected to pay the debt?'

'Indeed it was,' my father said. 'Not a single penny was left due and Father Owen had money spared after clearing the debts.'

'He was surely worth that!' said Muiris.

'No lie there!' from my father. 'A fortnight after Court Day word was sent out to the parishioners to solve the difficulty in which Father Owen found himself. Everyone knew that the difficulty in question was the costs of the law-case so they were fully determined to do their best to help him. Church gate collections were held the following Sunday and each parish rivalled the other to see which would win a word of praise from Father Owen. Thus, a good deal more was subscribed than was needed to clear the debts.

46

'Long life to you!' said Jim, 'I never before heard that story about Father Owen.'

'Maybe so,' said my father. 'There was no end to his goodness as a clergyman and it was a pity that he died so early and in the bloom of his life.'

'May his glory in Heaven increase,' said Muiris. 'When the call came, he had to answer it.'

'Indeed he had to answer it,' said my father, 'and there was great mourning for him in the parish of Dingle!'

'True!' said Jim, 'and in the whole of Kerry too.'

'You've shortened this part of the night, Tomás,' said Muiris. 'You have a wonderful memory.'

'I think, Muiris,' said my father, 'that since I was seven years of age I never heard a thing I was interested in, that isn't inside in my head this day as clear as the first day I heard it.'

They took out their pipes then, and my word to you but they knocked steam out of them. I'd say that this was the very first little tale that I ever memorized and it remained firmly embedded in my head until this very day.

When they had the pipes smoked, Muiris said it was time to be going home, and off they went. Cáit was home a short time before Seán, and when he came, all of us went on our knees and we recited the Rosary.

My father went to the door. 'I declare,' he said, 'but it's late enough now. The Plei-a-des are in the west above Coum Hill.'

'Nothing for it so,' said Cáit, 'but to pass away a bit of the morning as well.'

'Fine and easy, you have it, my girl! Did you ever hear about the woman in the olden times who said it was a great shame to waste God's light while one was asleep and to use the boor's light while one was awake.'

'Bad cess to her,' said Cáit. 'She died too, and there's many a light burned after her since she went.'

'Death is before everyone,' my father said, 'and no one will live forever. But in any event, it's time, and overtime, to go to bed now.'

The Day of the Races

*Taking to the road — Old people who were still supple! —
A day for drink and a great day for music! — Such Races
were never seen! — How we reached the town — A tipsy,
merry night*

I went to school the following Monday morning for as
yet I wasn't finished with the place. But, to tell you the
truth, my mind wasn't on a single thing except the Races.
All the other lassies had the same story; they were as
merry as could be—that is, those who were old enough
to go to Races. From day to day we were waiting and at
long last the great day dawned. Amongst ourselves we
were pondering and considering how we'd dodge off
from school—or would we get a free day from the Master?
But the evening before, when he was on the point of
leaving us home, he went round the school with a fistful
of pennies; to anyone of the scholars of an age to travel to
the Races under his own steam, he gave a shilling to the
bigger children and sixpence to the others.

'Attend school in the morning,' he told us, 'and when
the Rolls are called I'll give ye a free day!'

Oh boys, oh boys, didn't we suddenly sprout wings!
Isn't youth a funny thing! It's easy to coax it because as
the saying goes: 'Give a child something and back he'll
come tomorrow.' We were only too anxious to attend
school that morning, although many of us were slow and
lazy afterwards.

You can take it from me that on the morning of the
Races there wasn't a wink of sleep in our eyes. I myself
was out of bed at the crack of dawn and the sun was a
beautiful sight as it raised its brilliant amber head from
behind the Clasach. Back I went to Cáit-Jim: she was
still asleep.

'Bad manners to you, Cáit,' I said, 'are you asleep yet?'
She stirred herself.

'Isn't it early you're here!' she said.

'Didn't the Master tell us yesterday to be at school very early?' I answered. 'Everyone will be going to the Races and there'll be no one to go with us unless he lets us home early.'

'Don't be a bit worried,' Jim said, ''twill be a long while yet this day before the horses start running and 'twill be time and plenty to face southwards about twelve o'clock.'

'Welcome be God's help!' I said. 'They'll be with us so?'

'Aye, girl,' said Jim. 'Off home with you now and eat a bite of food; these here will be ready immediately.' All the children were squabbling and getting ready for school.

When I arrived home the breakfast was prepared before me and indeed I couldn't eat much of it because of the excitement bubbling over in my heart.

When we reached the school the Master was there before us: he didn't teach us many rules that day but gave us our freedom at eleven o'clock.

'I'll be with ye as ye go south,' he told us.

When I came back to the house my father was ready before me. 'Isn't Jim taking a long time to arrive?' he said. But it wasn't long until I saw him striding towards me from the west. 'He's coming, I assure you,' I said, 'and boy, he's travelling all out!'

My mother, the poor woman, was sitting in the corner not knowing what was going on but when she saw me as giddy as a goat around the house she said: 'What's pinching you now, Featherhead?'

'I'm off to the Races, girl,' said I.

'To the Races?' she echoed in surprise. 'Who'll be with you?'

'My father and Cáit-Jim.'

'Well, well, you have a right mark depending on your Da—the biggest ninnyhammer in the country when he has a drop taken!'

'I don't care,' I said. 'He won't get drunk at all, because Jim and Old Muiris will be with him.'

She gave a hearty laugh.

'God help your head, child,' she said. 'They're lick alike the pair of them, for one is as light-headed as th' other. Don't depend on your Da because by the end of the day he won't remember that you were ever with him.'

'Don't worry! There'll be other people there with me.'

'God prosper your day, child,' she said then.

Off with us down the road and who should be coming from the west but Frawley and he was in a great hurry.

'One extra and no one less!' said Muiris. 'Are you heading for the Races, Paddy Frawley?'

'Dead right, my little darling,' said Paddy. 'Isn't it many a day we'll spend in the graveyard, a place where our gums won't ask for food.'

'Right!' said Jim. 'And no one will cast a thought on us either.'

We headed away up past *Tobar a' Chéirín* and who was before us at the mouth of the bohareen but the Master. He saluted us and we returned his salute in like manner. I was class of shy and so was Cáit-Jim because he was teaching us at school but just the same he was very kind to us. We had travelled east as far as Hare Rock when Frawley spoke up.

'Oyeh, my darling, now or never our luck is in! Since the Master is with us we're not likely to be thirsty.'

'You'll have a pint, whatever,' said the Master.

'That you may never see a poor day, my sweet man,' said the other fellow. Frawley was a strong robust man and a good man in company too. We didn't feel the time passing while he was with us because he started to tell the Master how he had spent his early days.

'You hadn't it too good, I daresay?' the Master asked.

'I'd put a lie on my soul if I said I had it good. I was crooked and I was straight, but I didn't let my children die with the hunger whatever way the wind blew!'

'You weren't called out of your name, so!' said the Master.

'How's that?' Paddy asked.

'That you were a good robber, indeed!'

'In the full presence of the Lord God, my darling man, open confession is good for the soul. Although I never took a penn'orth from a poor man, I often whipped a great lump of loot from the ill-bred upstarts that could well afford it.'

'I suppose,' said the Master rising him again, 'that you found it hard to get absolution from the priest for all this robbery.'

Frawley started laughing.

'Listen to me, man,' he said, 'I was living here west in the cabin and I got an attack of erysipelas, and to make matters worse where did it strike me but right across my two eyes. I was a living example of misery, without light by day or by night and you'd think that my head was one big lump of dough. I was real bad and I had to send for the priest. Father Liam, God grant him a bed in heaven, was in Ballyferriter at the time and when he arrived at the cabin there was a great mob of people inside. To prove to you that I'm not telling lies there are witnesses here beside me; because each one of these three was in the house at that time,' Paddy added, indicating the others present.

'Correct!' said Jim.

'There you are!' said Paddy. 'And that's although I have the reputation of being a liar as well as a thief.'

'*Erra*, man,' said the Master, driving him further, 'no one was ever an accomplished man who wasn't crooked and straight. But what about the priest?'

'Oh,' said Paddy, 'he wanted to hunt out the people, but I told him to let them alone—that it made no difference to me whether they were in the house or not. "I suppose, Father," I said, "that I'm for the long road and I'll have to take my stand before a sterner Judge than these. I never let my children die with the hunger, Father!" I went on, "although there was hunger and want there in my time. The bad times had a firm hoult of the poor people and they were dying all bunched together in those days. But praise be to God, Father, I let none of mine die for the want of a bite. I was strong and able in those

51

days and it wasn't easy to catch up with me when I had the loot on board! But when those times passed and when we had full and plenty I turned my back on roguery. Then I was able to provide for my family from the sea and from the land. Now, Father, I daresay there's an end to my exploits and I fear the God of Glory as a witness to my deeds more than I do these here—but God have mercy on me whatever." "Amen!" said the Priest.'

'Did they stay inside?' the Master asked.

'Before God, darling,' said Paddy, 'I didn't give a damn whether they were inside or out because *they* weren't bothering me the most.'

With this talk of Frawley's we didn't find the journey long; by this time we were coming down over the top of the Long Road and I saw the Master making signs to Jim. 'You're going to play some practical joke now,' I said in my own mind.

As we were nearing Tomás Mhuirisín's house the Master said, 'As sure as my name is Seán Daly I'll give his bellyful of drink to the runner who'll be first at Togher River.'

'Adorable man, by God, it's a bargain! I suppose you won't renege in your word?' Paddy said.

'No fear!' said the Master. Then he set all three standing together on the crown of the road—Paddy, Muiris and my father.

'When I give the order,' said the Master, 'get moving!'

They were only waiting for the wind of the word.

'Go!' said the Master. And off they went with the fall of ground down the Long Road knocking sparks out of the stones. Paddy had the lead of the other two and when he found himself completely clear of them he'd give this cat's look over his shoulder to see if they were far behind. The three men carried on with the race until they reached Togher River but I assure you that Paddy held his lead and won the bet.

When we came up to them the three old men were seated on the edge of the road with sweat pouring down off them.

'My love forever!' said the Master catching Paddy by the hand. 'True for you to say a while ago that there was life in your feet and that it wasn't easy to catch up with you.'

'The man who'd catch me in my prime never stood in shoe leather,' said Paddy, 'and that's in the presence of my Maker!'

'You're a fit man yet,' said Muiris.

'That he is,' said the Master, 'and he has earned a drink.'

When they had recovered their breath and their hearts had stopped pounding we moved off down the road. When we reached the strand every square inch of it was covered with standings and platforms. Tables laden down with sweet cakes and confectionery were laid out and the thimble-riggers and the people who supplied food had tables too.

The Master called his own company into a booth where drink was on sale. 'Sit into the table!' he ordered.

When they were seated comfortably he called for a gallon of porter and planked it down in front of Frawley. He gave him a glass with which to measure it out for drinking.

'Here, Paddy,' he said. 'Dole that out among these men and drink my health.'

'May you never see a poor day!' said Paddy. 'It's no lie to call you a big-hearted man.' The Master drank only one drink. 'Good luck, now!' he said, 'I'll be off to join my own crowd!'

Cáit-Jim and myself were sitting on a little bench near the head of the table enjoying some apples we had bought before we went in.

By the time the gallon can was empty the men were getting a little bit noisy; Muiris rapped on the table and the barmaid arrived.

'What do you want?' she asked.

'Fill up that, my good woman,' he ordered.

She wanted only the merest hint. She took away the can and before very long she came back with yellow froth on

53

the brim of that same vessel. The men went from drink to drink until none of them knew whether he was standing on his head or heels.

More and more people kept crowding into the booth until in the end it was packed to overflowing. Then the hullabaloo and noise began: one man was praising, another was dispraising and a third was going clean out of his mind singing.

Before very long I heard Jim, a pint of porter in his hand, singing in a low sweet voice.

> *Bad luck to the naggin measure!*
> *I never thought it a treat*
> *—What I'd offer a child for pleasure*
> *Who'd follow me down the street*
> *But spirits poured out in full quarts*
> *Are my choice on a generous table,*
> *For I'd drink with the best of good sports*
> *And cry 'Health!' the while I was able.*
>
> *And I have a news to narrate*
> *That I'll spread at the top of my voice,*
> *For as whiskey grows cheaper by rate*
> *My heartstrings have cause to rejoice.*
> *To the true men my story's worth knowing*
> *From the head of the table they're beckoning.*
> *—We'll get whiskey in bumpers o'erflowing*
> *And three months for to settle the reckoning!*

He carried on like this and when he was well and truly tipsy you could hear his voice if you were away down below the graveyard. Anyway, the finish he had to his song was:

> *But why complain when the future's dim*
> *For our love is the jug that's full to the brim!*

They were all tangled up in each other like this for a while; before long I saw a big, tall, middle-aged man pressing in through the people and he never stopped until he reached my father's side. As soon as my father saw him coming he got up and gave him a right hearty greeting. When Jim heard the welcome he said:

'Well, well, Seán, you're welcome a thousand times over!'

'Long live the company in the whole of its health!' said Seán in reply. 'When I heard ye were here nothing would do me but to join ye.'

'Aha, my boy,' said my father, 'blood knows blood!'

'Dead right!' said Seán and he rapped on the table. When the barmaid arrived, 'Send us in a pint of whiskey,' said Seán.

It wasn't long till she was back with a full jug of whiskey; down she laid it on the table directly in front of Seán.

'Here now, grand-uncle,' Seán said to my father, 'divide that out among the company.'

Indeed and indeed, when the hot drop got under their teeth it played Molly Bawn to them entirely, because everyone then had his voice raised until there was no knowing who was best or who was worst. Seán caught my father's hand and told him to sing a song.

'Put it on my soul,' said my father, 'but I have a hoarseness in my throat from howling since morning.'

Seán filled out a glass for him: 'Here!' he said, 'that will banish your hoarseness!'

My father knocked back the drink very smartly indeed; then he gripped Seán's hand and raised his voice in the following verses:

> *Black green this bough of ivy*
> *Without blemish, without woe;*
> *Sunnier grows the summer now,*
> *On the tree-crest, a dark crow.*
> *—Her neat delicate waistline,*
> *Her honey-mouth compelling,*
> *By the bridge above the green sward*
> *My true love has her dwelling.*

55

I was a champion sleánsman
And better still on the loy;
My right arm with the flail striking
On the threshing-floor in joy.
—I will leave my habitation,
My world is upside down,
And follow my ringletted darling
Wherever her track be found.

Had I the wings of a seabird,
Grown from my shoulders both,
I would scale the airs of heaven
As high as the cliffs on the coast.
—With my bitter complaint I would travel
To seek my dearest brother,
For my hundred-love has betrayed me
And her name is linked with another.

Time was slipping away and I was getting weary for I had a headache from all the noise.

'It looks as if we'll be here all night, Cáit-Jim,' I said. 'If only we could steal out . . . If only I did as my mother advised in the morning for she was right when she told me that it was the most foolish thing in the world to depend on my father.'

'Tell him we're going away out,' Cáit-Jim said.

I went over to him and I was crying class of pettishly.

'Are you going home at all, Dad?' I asked him.

'Home we'll go, with the help of God! Don't be one bit uneasy about that.' he said.

'Is that your little girl, Tomás?' Seán asked.

'Mine she is, son! The scrapings of the pot!'

Seán brought me over close beside his knee; he put his hand into his pocket and gave me a half-crown. I was delighted.

'Who's that man, Dad?' I asked my father.

'Seán Sayers, one great-hearted soul from Kilcooly,' he answered.

'Myself and Cáit-Jim are going out and maybe we'd

56

see my brother, Seán, and he'll be with us on the road home. But whisper! When will *you* go home?'

'I'll go home, a-girl, when I have enough drank,' he said. 'If you see Seán, go home with him and don't be depending on me.'

I left him there in the height of his glory chanting *Dónal na Gréine* and Cáit-Jim and myself went away. We weren't a bit hungry because there were plenty sweet-cakes and sweets there on the tables. 'Twasn't long until we met Seán.

'Where's your father?' he asked.

'Inside over there and a proper noody-nahdy he is,' I said.

'Tck-tck!' Seán said, 'that's the way he generally is. We'll be going home straightaway, girl.'

'I have a lot of pennies, Seán, and I'll give 'em to you for I don't need them except to bring a share of sweets to the little ones who couldn't come to the Races.'

We went over to the table directly opposite us and bought a share of sweets and cakes. I gave the balance of the money to Seán. Then we started out on the long road home. There was a great crowd of people with us but they have nothing to do with my story. Some of them were nice and tipsy, thus we didn't find the road long as we moved up the Clasach.

When we reached the house, it was late enough in the evening. As soon as we came in my mother welcomed us but Seán didn't sit down at all because he had to go after the horse above in the field.

'Aye!' said my mother. 'You must have a great lot of news after the Races. Did you see the horses run?'

''Pon my very soul, but I didn't,' I said, 'nor even a piece of a horse.'

That was true for me; from the start to the finish of the day, I never laid eyes on a horse nor a jockey but inside in a tent listening to the addled music of those men and my father. Neither, of course, did they cast a thought on a horse or a race.

'Where did you leave the Forest Ranger?' she asked again.

'There's a crowd of them coming after us,' I replied—this because I didn't want to leave my father holding the dirty end of the stick.

'He was merry, I suppose, if he was running true to form,' she said.

'Everyone there was on his ear, girl.' I replied.

'May God send us cause to laugh,' she said. 'Nobody is ever in a right hobble except the one who hasn't the use of her legs.'

When Cáit came in after milking the cows I gave my mother and herself some of the sweets; the rest I gave to the neighbouring youngsters who had come in. They were well satisfied.

By this time night had fallen and my father wasn't yet home. A fine red fire glowed on the hearthstone and a pot of potatoes hung above it. Very soon I heard the tatterara coming up the road.

'They're coming!' I said and I was all agog.

Before long my father came in the door: he was as light in his head as a puck goat and he was singing:

'Óró, Old Man, With You I Won't Go' . . .

When my mother saw him she said, 'Bad scran to you, how well you never lost the old habit!'

He moved up to her and out of his pocket he took a half-pint of whiskey and held it out to her.

'Here, drink my health,' he said, 'and let Cáit do likewise.'

'May I never lose you!' said my mother. 'My word, but you never forgot me! Bring me up the little cup, Cáit.'

She poured a lively drop out of the bottle.

'Drink my health now, Cáit Boland,' she told her daughter-in-law and she drank another spill of it, herself. Then there was peace between them.

We barely had the potatoes eaten when Jim and Muiris landed in the door.

'Bygor,' Muiris said, 'we couldn't shut an eye without paying a visit.'

They didn't come empty-handed either for each

brought a drop to my mother. Because of the fact that she hadn't her health they never forgot her! I dodged out unknown to the rest and raced across the river to Seán Bán's house where my brother Pádraig was sitting inside before me.

'Any news from the Races?' he asked.

'The dickens to it, Pádraig!' I said. 'Come over and have sport for a while of the night since you weren't at the Races.'

He came quickly to his feet even though he was lame as a result of a pain in his leg. Over we went; I let him in before me and I lingered behind for a good bit.

As soon as he came in my mother gave him a welcome and a half. She took her bottle and held it out to him.

'Drink that, son, since you weren't able to go to the Races!' she said.

By this time my father was raising every second bar of a song. Indeed, dear reader, it was the same as being at a wedding as listening to the company I had that night, for we had dancing and music and we sang all the fine lively old Irish songs.

My mother was the finest singer that ever sang a verse of a song. Although she was in poor health she relished company, and now that she had a little drop on board Muiris asked her to sing. The song she sang was *Gráinne Mhaol* and when that was finished Pádraig began *An Clár Bog Déil*. They carried on like this until midnight.

I think that was the most entertaining night I ever spent at the start of my days.

The Same Old Story Ever
and Always

*A day out of home minding my brother's house — This irks
another — 'Let her go to some other house!' — My father
recalls the Famine — The corpse that fell through the coffin*

'GRASP opportunity when it offers,' that's an old saying
of which I have had experience.

The following day—it was Saturday—I got up early as
the morning was very fine and when I had my breakfast
eaten Cáit told me to go down minding the cows and to
let Seán home to his breakfast.

The morning was fine and sunny; it was about nine
o'clock when she called on me to drive the cows home. I
drove them out before me until I reached the end of the
little fence; there I heard Máire Bhán, Pádraig's wife,
calling to me from the other house so I went over to her.

'What do you want me for?' I asked.

'Maybe you'd mind Bríghde till I come home?'

'Where are you off to?'

'We're going to Dingle. You won't have a whole lot to
do. My father will boil the potatoes for the pigs.'

I was about thirteen and a half at that time and I was
able for a lot of little jobs around the house.

As soon as they were ready, they went off to Dingle; it
was late enough in the evening when they arrived home.

We had a fine glowing fire on the hearth. To see a grain
of tea at that time was a great rarity but Máire brought
some back from Dingle and then she wet the tea. She
gave me a chunk of baker's bread and a cup of tea; I was
satisfied when my stomach was full and I had a share of
sweets into the bargain.

When everything was tidied up I rambled off home,

but alas! as I was making for the door I heard the argument going on inside.

'The same old story ever and always,' I told myself, for Cáit, my brother's wife, was inside with her voice pitched high in anger.

'Let her go to some other house besides this one!' she said. 'I am not going to be cooking for her while she's working for other people.'

From that I realized that I was the subject of the argument and I stole in with a heavy heart. I sat in the corner and took down my little bag of books. The other lady and my father were swapping every second angry word but I never pretended that I heard them although I wasn't reading. Nor was my mind on the book but on the life that lay ahead of me. However, Muiris came in and that put a stop to the snarling.

You'd never imagine then that there had ever been the slightest disagreement between the pair of them because they started to discuss the affairs of the world. They were referring to 'The Bad Times' and my father had some wonderful anecdotes to tell about those same evil days for he could recall every single detail concerning them.

'Sixteen years of age I was, Muiris,' he said, 'when my uncle died with the hunger. He had three in family; they were grown up and whatever bit of food was going he preferred to give it to the family so as to keep them alive, but God help us, he failed! The world was too hard. He himself was the first to die; he was a big, strong man but he couldn't live without food. Hunger got the upperhand of him and he died.

'In those days there was neither coffin nor sheet to cover poor people nor was there anyone to shoulder their bodies to the graveyard. But my father got some old boards—he and a pair of men from the same townland—and they knocked the boards together to make a class of a coffin. They put the unfortunate corpse into it. I was the fourth of the bearers and I was under the front of the coffin. The big farmyard was on a height and whatever misfortune was down on top of me, my heels struck a stone that lay in my path—this because I was moving backwards down by the side of the house. We hadn't sufficient room to move, so the two legs were taken from under me and I was capsized below in the dung-heap with coffin and corpse after me. I own to God and the world,' he went on, 'that that was the day I got the biggest fright of my life. When I lifted my head the coffin had fallen asunder and the feet of the corpse were sticking out before me.'

'A terrible sight!' said Muiris.

'God grant that Christian people may never again experience that sort of life!'

'Amen!' said Muiris.

'We had to get a couple of ropes and tie them round the coffin to see if we could manage to take it to the graveyard. My uncle's wife and family didn't live long afterwards; the cabin tumbled down on top of their heads and I remember that at that time four houses in our townland met the same end.'

'Anyone living then was to be pitied,' Muiris said.

'I declare that my blood shivers when I recall it,' said my father. 'The bad times destroyed this land and wiped out the population.'

'Hey, man!' Muiris said, 'isn't that how the big farmers came by all the land they have today!'

''Twas easy to get it that time,' my father said.

'Time to go home,' said Muiris. 'Good night to ye!' And off he went.

Farewell to My Youth

My father's trip to Dingle — A place in service for me in Dingle — My last morning at school

THE following day was a Sunday and everybody was doing his best to get ready for Mass, but when I got out of bed my father was nowhere to be seen. After we came home from Mass, dinner was ready, but there was still no trace of my father nor did anyone know where he had gone to. About six o'clock in the evening he strolled in the door.

'May the morning hoarseness catch you!' said my mother. 'Where were you all day?'

'In Dingle.'

'What did you want there for?'

'To get some place that'd suit that chubby lassie there!'

'And did you get it?'

'There's a place for her in Séamas Curran's house. Don't be a bit uneasy: Nell will be as good as a mother to her.'

'And God help me,' said my mother in a troubled tone of voice, 'what will *I* do?'

'The very best you can, my good woman,' said my father. 'And if there's peace when she's gone so much the better for everyone.'

My mother said no more but put down her head and cried bitterly.

Young as I was, my heart almost broke when I realized what she would have to go through when I was far away from her. I slipped out of the house and went back to the garden; there I sat down and cried my fill. I wasn't thinking of sport nor of play at that time but of the time that lay before me. I was jealous of Cáit-Jim and of the

63

other girls who were as happy as the days are long, playing away for themselves. I thought that the turns of the world are very strange: some people sorrowful and others full of joy. At that particular moment the heart in my breast was broken with sorrow and dissatisfaction. I told myself that if everyone who had a brother's wife in the house was as heart-scalded as I was, then they were all very much to be pitied. My brother, Seán, was a good man but he wore only one leg of the britches.

It was getting late and I came in home; the food was on the table but I didn't eat much of it. Not a syllable out of anyone! They were all subdued, but when the time came for Muiris to arrive he came right in the door and Jim with him. They were chatting and making conversation for a while but they made no great delay because Muiris had a cold.

When my father got the house to himself and the rest were asleep: 'Go to school in the morning, child,' he told me, 'I have to talk to the schoolmaster about you.'

I didn't say a word but drew a sigh. I said my prayers and went to bed. But alas! I didn't get much sleep as I was weighing up the pros and cons of things the whole night long.

Apparently, I must have fallen asleep some time during the night, for it was bright morning when I awoke. I lifted the bedclothes from my head and looked directly in front of me. A sunbeam was coming through the window and a thousand midges were flitting here and there. I kept watching them and before long I saw a spider spinning a thread of slender silk out of his own body and lowering himself from the tie-beam of the rafters. On the bushes outside the little birds were singing sweetly. I heard the cock crowing gaily; he reminded me of the little tale my mother used tell me some time previously. She had asked me: 'What does the cock say when he crows?'

'I haven't the faintest idea,' I answered.

This is what she said then: 'When Christ's body was

placed in the grave the Jews told each other that the Joiner's Son, when He was alive, had boasted that He would rise on the third day. "Maybe," they told each other, "His followers will steal His body and then claim that He has risen from the dead!" "Go," said the President, "and secure the flagstone at the mouth of the tomb." When they had the flagstone well secured they came back and then made a feast and had a celebration. A pot of cockerels was boiling over the fire. "Did you do your business properly?" the President asked and one of the men concerned answered, "Never will He rise until the bird now boiling at the bottom of the pot rises from the dead." This was no sooner said than the cock rose to the edge of the pot, clapped his wings together and called out to the Son of Mary, "*Mac na hÓighe slán!* The Son of the Virgin is safe!" That's what the cock says when he crows,' my mother said.

I recalled that little story as I listened to the cock crowing.

'The High King of Creation be praised and thanked,' I said, 'Who ordained a livelihood for every creature according to nature! Whatever God has in store for me —that will come to pass!' With that I jumped out of bed.

When I was dressed, I washed my face and hands. I hadn't broken my fast but that made no difference for it wasn't the first time I had gone to school on an empty stomach. When I was ready I took my little bag of books and went down the road. I was only barely in time for school as the Rolls were being called as I went in. The Master looked at me out of a corner of his eye but never said a word.

An hour afterwards the latch on the door was lifted and my father came in. I knew well that the time had come and cold sweat broke out through me. My schooldays were over.

My father had a chat with the Master; after a while the teacher came over to me.

'Your father wants you,' he said in a kindly tone. 'Good luck to you, girl!'

I couldn't speak a word because I was too lonely. My

65

father went off out and I followed him. I'm telling you no lie when I say that there was a lump in my throat as I went home.

As soon as I went in—'Put on your clothes now,' my father said.

'Wait until I eat a bite anyway!' I answered.

I took some food and then put on my clothes. I caught my shawl and looked up towards the corner at my mother who was seated by the fire. Her body was huddled up and she was crying softly. I ran towards her and put my two arms around her.

My father had to come and take me away.

The New Life

*Walking to Dingle — Sights I never thought existed — Nell —
New friends — The brush — 'We'll both be thankful to each
other by-and-by' — Killing the pigs*

WE took the short cut east across the hill and went down
the Clasach; I had never before travelled that road except
on the day of the Races. When I got as far as Ventry it
seemed to me that everything and every place was
strange and queer. In the course of the journey I asked
my father a lot of questions and at last we reached Dingle.

But, oh dear me, a thousand times over, that's the
place that filled me with wonder! Grand tall buildings
stood on all sides of me and people were passing each
other backwards and forwards and I couldn't understand
one word of what they were saying. The two eyes were
popping out of my head with fright. 'God of Miracles!'
I told myself, 'I won't live one single day here!'

By this time we had reached the house we were bound
for. My father went in before me and I brought up the
rear.

'Welcome!' said the woman of the house. 'So ye're
here!'

'We are, Nell,' my father said.

'Into the kitchen with ye!' she said, going in ahead of us.

'Don't be a bit shy, girl,' she told me. 'You'll want for
nothing in this house.'

Nell made the tea; shop-bread and jam were put
before us and I assure you that I made the bread crackle
for I was hungry enough.

'You wash the cups and saucers now, Margaret,' she
told me and when I had hung the delph on the dresser,
'Take the brush and sweep the kitchen.'

Man alive, I never saw the likes of that for a brush

67

before, for what we used as a brush at home was a long handful of twigs, or a bush of heather with a sally rod twisted around it. However, I did my best.

'All right, girl,' she said. 'We'll both be thankful to each other by-and-by.'

How right she was, for I came to have as much affection for her as I had for my own mother. She was a generous, hospitable, pleasant woman and Séamas, her husband, was every bit as good as her. He took my father's place for four long years afterwards.

They had four in family, two sons and two daughters and that was the family that had the blessing of God about them. The eldest boy was eleven years of age and I don't think I ever saw as gentle a boy from that day to this.

There was an old woman in the house too—the boss's mother—Nan we called her. My father was related to her and because of this she was very friendly disposed towards me.

They kept a very busy shop that had a great country following. They sold almost everything, including articles that had to do with farming and agriculture, and also fishing gear of all kinds, tea and sugar as well, flour, meal, pork and many other commodities. And with that every class of drink was available there. It was one of the shops that did the best business in Dingle.

After part of the evening had passed by, my father got up. 'It's as well for me to be shortening the road west,' he said. 'Be a good girl now,' he added, turning to me, 'and let your mistress have no fault to find with you.'

'I won't have any fault to find,' Nell said in reply. 'Have no fear on that score.'

'So! The blessing of God be with ye,' my father said and off he went.

I was now alone in a strange house where I knew no one; worse still I knew no English except an odd word here and there that made no sense. But I was lucky, for Nan knew no English either. The adults in the house always spoke

Irish among themselves except when they were addressing the family.

When night fell they all came together in the kitchen: I was backward among them at first but soon I struck up a friendship with Seáinín, the eldest son, and with Anna, the daughter. Before long we were all fairly attached to one another and then I was on the pig's back!

By ten o'clock we were on our way to bed: the woman of the house led me up the stairs to a room in which there were two beds.

'There's your bed, now,' she told me. 'The other one is Nan's. You won't be lonely because you'll have her as company.'

'Very well,' I said.

I went on my knees and said my prayers but no thought of sleep nor of rest crossed my mind but the thought of my poor mother who was lonely after me. A bout of grief came over me and I started to cry. But at long, long last sleep overcame me as I was exhausted after the journey and I didn't open an eye until the man of the house called me in the morning.

I assure you, dear reader, that this was one time I didn't turn a deaf ear to the call for I was subject to discipline now and I had to be prepared. I had the kettle boiling when Nell got up. She didn't have a sulky face on her either; on the contrary she was bright and cheerful. We ate the breakfast and I was busy arranging everything for the children who were going off to school.

Before long I knew the run of the place—this because Seáinín was generally at my side and he'd explain the ins and outs of every task to me. Meanwhile, I was putting down my time: one day easy and another hard so that I never felt the time slipping by.

Fair Day came and the man of the house was in need of two or three pigs for killing so as to sell the pork to the customers for Christmas. He bought four pigs; the day they were being killed I was in a right panic for I had never before seen an animal being slaughtered. Fat

Séamas was the name of the pig-sticker and he was a real bitter boyo especially when he had a drop taken. He had a drop taken that day and you wouldn't relish it if he looked at you with fury in his eyes. He was a stout, sallow, middle-aged man.

There was a table in the back garden on top of which the pig was to be placed. The man of the house and Séamas tied up the pig and landed her on top of the table. Nell called myself.

'Bring the basin with you, Margaret,' she said, 'and hold it under the blood.'

I caught the basin and went to the table.

'Hold it properly now!' Séamas said.

Erra, man dear, I had the tremor in all my limbs. When he stuck the knife into the pig's throat she let this unmerciful screech out of her that knocked echoes out of the place! But if she did, I let go a screech every bit as loud and the basin dropped out of my two hands and fell to the ground.

'Hold the vessel right you thunderin' *straip* or I'll give you what I'm givin' the pig!' said Fat Séamas.

Reader dear, I assure you that he put the heart crossways in me with his two wild eyes and his long knife and I did my level best to hold the basin properly. But by the time the last of the pigs was dead, all my fears had vanished.

One Friday after dinnertime there was no one in the shop; the man of the house was looking after cattle and Nell and myself were in the kitchen. She was ironing clothes when there was a knock on the door outside.

'Go out, Margaret girl, and see if there's anyone outside!' she told me.

When I went out to the shop I could see no one, so I gave a quick glance down into the room. A man was standing behind the door and he struck me as being kind of queer.

'What do you want, my good man?' I asked him.

He looked at me with an unnatural stare in his eyes.

'Bring me a fourpenny glass of whiskey!'

I went in. 'There's a frightening old fellah outside the

room door and he told me to bring him a fourpenny glass of whiskey,' I told Nell.

'Come on out!' she said.

She went out into the shop and filled up the glass. She gave a quick eye down at the room door and plainly saw the man who was below. She handed me the glass.

'Don't give it to him until you get the money,' she said.

I was surprised to hear her speak like that for she was a charitable, generous woman.

I stood directly in front of the man with the glass in my hand. 'Decent man,' I said, 'my orders are: not to give you the drink until I get the money.'

He looked at the glass and then he looked at me and the look he gave me is still branded on my heart and mind. He put his hand into the pocket of his old britches and he was searching for a while. He found the fourpenny piece and handed it to me.

I gave him the glass then. God save us! his hand was trembling and his mouth was gaping open. Almost before the glass had touched his lips at all he had swallowed its contents and it gurgled as it went back his throat. He wiped his mouth with the palm of his hand and went out. I came over to Nell with the fourpence and the empty glass in my hand—she was still in the shop.

'That fellow gone out terrified me,' I said. 'I never saw anyone like him as long as I'm in this house. And what a death he gave that glassful!'

I saw the tears running down her face.

'God help us!' she said. 'That same drink has him the way he is. That man was one of the most independent men in the town of Dingle and no one was in the public eye more than Small Tom, his father. That man out was all the family he had and what a tremendous fuss there was the day he married a merchant's daughter in the great town of Tralee. The churchbells of the two towns were ringing for him on his wedding day—and look at him now,' she went on, 'hasn't he a godforsaken appearance?'

'God help us, Nell,' I said. 'Isn't drink a curse?'

'It is, pet, for the person who has too much of a mind for it.'

That evening Nell sent off the fourpence to a relative of the unfortunate man for she would have nothing whatsoever to do with the money.

Often afterwards in the course of the year I saw the same man and he looked frightful. He and his family of three were evicted out of house and home. I have no idea what happened to the family but he himself died under some kind of a shelter at the top of John Street.

Whenever Séamas, the boss of the house, came home he usually had a number of interesting stories to tell but I didn't pay him much attention because I had jobs to do around the house.

The days were moving on. I was satisfied at times—at other times I wasn't satisfied at all. When night-time came I didn't lack company for the people of the house were certainly pleasant to me; it was mostly from Nan that Seáinín and myself drew entertainment for she had a habit of telling us funny little stories. I'd spend part of the night teaching the two girls and before long they had a share of Irish. In return for my teaching them Irish they'd teach me English. The man of the house would have a newspaper and he'd often tell me:

'Always read the papers, Margaret, and you'll never forget your learning.'

That's the way we'd pass the night until it was time for sleep.

Christmastide

My first Christmas far from home — The young family of the house — Christian joy — Nan's tale about the Blessed Lamb — I recite 'The Welcome of the Child Jesus' for them

BY this time Christmas was not far away and this is the time of greatest hustle and bustle for townspeople. On the Saturday before Christmas the street was black with people: they were like harvest midges moving in and out through each other, collecting 'commands' as they went from house to house and a good number of the men with their hats on the sides of their heads as a result of their having a jorum taken. I thought that there weren't so many people in the world as were gathered into the house at that hour of day! Such argument and uproar and discussion! The taproom was a solid mass of people; in the middle of the floor stood a great long table with forms on either side of it and the people were so crushed together that a tiny wren wouldn't have found room to move among them. One man was singing and another was talking: I wasn't listening to anyone but to Micil Thomáisín singing *Bó na bPúcaí*—'The Fairy Cow'—a song made by Poet Dunlea. This was a song mocking the peelers:

> *A Captain Cinders who ne'er saw battle*
> *From Ballygoleen despatched with cattle*
> *A pair of peelers with strict citation*
> *To make 'Ferriter Dunes their destination.*
> *On their journey there they passed resolution*
> *At Tavern Hoare to make dissolution*
> *And while they'd loiter and have their spree*
> *On the road the cattle could wander free.*

73

Every time he finished a verse the rest of the company would raise this yell that'd knock echoes out of the loft over their heads. After a while a man stuck down his head.

'I own to God, Micil,' he said, 'wouldn't a scrap o' sense be better to you than that nourishment! The Brass Buttons are outside!'

'Let them go to hell, son,' Micil said, and he raised his voice in another verse:

> *As they entered the bar and the maid instructed*
> *The Gentle People a cow abducted;*
> *With magical hues they began to size her*
> *Till no peeler born could recognize her.*
> *They bore her aloft in a whirl of mist*
> *By breezes from Marhan and Clasach kissed.*
> *She now yields milk in creamy spillage*
> *In a fort to the north of O'Dorney Village.*

Before long Beit his wife, came in. 'Miraculous God!' she said, 'have any of ye seen this Micil of mine?'

'I'm here, girl; come on down,' said Micil.

She got a welcome and she took her seat at the end of the bench.

'You'll drink a drop now,' said Micil, 'and then we'll head for home.'

'Wisha,' says Beit, 'isn't it bad enough for one of us to be cracked without having the pair of us in the one trim.'

Micil stood up and filled a glass out of a jug that stood on the table. Beit was trying to refuse the drink.

'Here, girl!' he said raising another blast of a song:

> *Your health, my friend, and drain your glass*
> *Our common welfare will come to pass!*

and he began his song all over again.

The peelers were busy outside because at that time there was great agitation among the people. The Land

74

Question was still very much to the fore and the unfortunate tenants were being sorely harried by the landlords. Like every other place a branch of the Land League had been established in Dingle and many people were starting to take part in the Plan of Campaign, and as a result of this, here and there a person was being boycotted. So the peelers had their hands full, especially in any locality where there were drinkers and spouters for they had the suspicion that whatever secret or privacy topers held they'd maybe let it slip out in their talk when their wits were astray. But take my word for it, the people were very cautious and they'd give the 'Brassies' the least opportunity possible.

However, Micil was in full cry when, in the final verse of the song, two policemen hopped in the door, and grabbing poor Micil, they hoisted him off to the barracks. That was the first person I had ever seen being arrested by the authorities.

The house was then like a grave; not a hum nor a haw out of anyone and those present began to drift off quietly. No one felt the situation as keenly as Beit because now she had no one to guide the horse home and she was troubled in her mind and very upset.

'Pull yourself together!' Séamas, the man of the house, told her. 'The night will be fine and bright and if all goes to all they can't keep him inside beyond ten o'clock. Muiris Bán and myself will go to the barracks and get him released at ten.' The poor woman calmed down then.

About ten o'clock Séamas and Muiris went off and brought Micil back with them. He was your subdued man! When he came in the door to us with a class of a foolish smirk on his face, Beit said, ''Tis easily known that your throat would land you in trouble, my hayro!'

'Shut up now!' said Micil. 'Can't I boast that I was taken to the barracks without any charge being laid against me except that I was singing! Get ready straight-away and believe you me, too, the black mare won't be long covering the road north.'

They said good-bye to us and I daresay they weren't idle until they reached home.

Christmas Eve fell on a Tuesday and everyone was busy preparing for it. Seáinín came in the door carrying a bundle of ivy and holly.

'Give me a hand, Margaret,' he said, 'till I fasten this to the window.'

'I know nothing about it,' I said, 'because I never saw it done.'

'You'll see it now, girl, and when it'll be fixed up it will be simply beautiful.'

Anna and Eibhlín were busy making paper flowers of every colour; according as they had a flower finished Seáinín would tuck it in among the ivy.

'Bring me the candle now,' he told me.

I got a great red candle and a candlestick; this he set on the window-sill.

'Make the tea, you,' he told me, 'while I'm fixing up the rest of it.'

I hung the kettle over the fire and while I was waiting for it to boil I fixed the table in the middle of the kitchen. Seáinín told me to get a blue candle, to light it and place it on the table. When I had it lighting I laid the table with delf for the tea. Then Nell got up, and bringing with her three kinds of bread, she sliced it on a bread board. There was plenty jam and butter on the table too and when all the lights were lighting and the kitchen was decorated I thought that I was in the Kingdom of Heaven because I had never before seen such a lovely sight. Nell poured out the tea and everyone sat down to the table; they were all pleasant and cheerful, especially Nell. Every single move her family made, filled her with joy.

I was watching them very closely as I drank my tea. Thoughts ran into my mind: I was thinking of my poor mother at that time. I knew the kind of a night she had, a near-sighted, lonely, unfortunate woman without light or joy for I was the one comfort she had in this life. I was far away from her now and I couldn't raise her spirits nor offer her a scrap of happiness.

'The way of the world is strange,' I told myself. 'Look at Nell and the comfort she draws from her family and there are other poor mothers who never get the slightest scrap of satisfaction out of life.'

In spite of all the pleasure around me tears came to my eyes. Seáinín noticed me. 'Margaret is lonesome,' he said.

He came over to me from the other side of the table and began to give me soft talk so as to take my mind off my loneliness.

'Seáinín,' I told him, 'I'm not a bit lonely in the way you imagine, but I was thinking of my mother. Go back and drink your tea.' Then I began eating just like he was.

When we had the supper eaten and all the things were set aside Séamas came in with a bottle of wine and a glass in his hand. 'Would ye like punch?' he asked us.

'We would, Daddy,' the children said. 'This is Christmas Eve!'

'I don't care for wine at all, darlin',' Nan said. 'I prefer a little drop of whiskey.'

Back he went and then returned with a jugful of whiskey.

'Here, take your pick of them!' he said.

Nell made a small drop of wine-negus that was suitable for the family and she gave me a fair jorum of it too.

'Won't you have a drop yourself, Missus?' I asked her.

'I won't, child,' she said. 'I never let a spoonful of drink pass my lips nor would I give it to these children but as little but for respect for the Night that's there.'

'Would you be afraid you'd get drunk?' I asked, for curiosity was picking me.

'Not that, child, but it has always been said: "Taste the food and you'll get fond of it." I don't think there was ever a person who was sipping and tipping at drink but got a mind for it in the latter end.'

Séamaisín and Eibhlín were over at the window-sill examining the small lovely pictures that Seáinín had placed here and there. Eibhlín took one of them in her hand and went over where Nan was.

'Nan,' she said, 'look at the nice little Lamb with His feet tied.'

'Aye,' said Nan, 'that's the Blessed Infant whom we all adore tonight.'

'Why does He take the shape of a lamb?' the child wanted to know.

'Sit down there quietly,' Nan said, 'and I'll tell you.'
They all sat down.

'At that time a king of high rank called Herod ruled the
district where Mary and the Infant were living. He heard
about the child Jesus and made up his mind to put to
death every male child under the age of three months. He
ordered his bodyguard and his soldiers to guard the
great city of Bethlehem and not to allow anyone in or
out without first finding out all about their business.
Immediately the order was received, sentries and guards
were posted in every street, at every street corner and on
every road and highway. Mary had a close friend called
Bríghde and when *she* heard the news she went to Mary
who, when she saw her coming, gave her a warm welcome.
"Mary," Bríghde told her, "this is no time for talking;
it's time to do a good deed." "What's the news now,
Bríghde?' Mary asked. "You surely must have heard the
dreadful command that Herod has issued? I've come to
see if I can think of any plan that will help you to save
Little Jesus from the strait He's in." "God will help us,
Bríghde," Mary answered. "Get ready so," said Bríghde,
"and make no delay. Before daylight in the morning I
will dress myself in an *óinseach's* rags and head for such
and such a street. Maybe those on guard will follow me;
if they do, face southward for the road that leads from
the city and perhaps you'll succeed in crossing the
bridge of the Great River before anyone challenges you.
Good-bye now; I'll be off about my business."

'When Joseph came in Mary told him the whole story
from start to finish. The following morning, as it was
brightening for day a terrible uproar could be heard
outside. A foolish woman was decked out in straw and
around her waist was a belt studded with lights and on
her head was a ring with twelve candles lighting upon it.
She made her way to the point most convenient for Mary
to escape. She had a kind of a flute that made an odd
sound: as she played the flute the guards were startled
and when they raised their heads they saw the witless
woman all lighted up. They went towards her, but she
kept moving away before them like a gust of wind.

'As soon as Mary got the guards out of the way she set about making her way out of the city. Things went well for her until she came to the bridge across the Great River and there were two soldiers of the guard: they stood right before her on the crown of the road.

'"Where are you off to so early, decent woman?" one of them asked.

'"I've been a week in the city," Mary answered, "and my home is a good distance away. That's why I'm on the road so early."

'"What's that load you have on your back?' a soldier asked again.

'"A little lamb I got to rear as a pet."

'"Maybe this is an excuse," said the other soldier seizing her and dragging her mantle off her. All he saw was a lamb, its four legs tied with a light cord.

'"See now; she's right," said the other soldier. "It's a great shame for us to delay her."

'Mary was walking on and on until she was free from danger; she sat down in a little corner under a green clump of bushes and lifted Jesus off her back. When she was rested she replaced Him on her back and some time later reached her destination. She now had the Infant safe; a few days afterwards there was appalling desolation and terror because of the slaughter of the little children of the city. The only sound to be heard was the sorrowful crying of the mothers whose children were being put to death by Herod the destroyer. When the dreadful scourge was over Bríghde went out to where Mary was and the pair of women were overjoyed at meeting each other again. They went on their knees and earnestly thanked God for having saved them. Mary could bestow no greater honour on Bríghde than to present her with a feastday. She did so in these words:

'"Your day will come before my day, Bríghde, until the end of the world."

'It has been thus ever since and Bríghde's Day comes before Mary's Day and, since there were candles in the plan that Bríghde thought of, candles are blessed in every church throughout the world; "Candlemas Day" it's called.'

'How I love the tiny Lamb!' Eibhlín said.

That love remained in the girl's heart ever afterwards for she offered herself up to the Merciful Lamb and became a nun.

I myself told Nell that Séamaisín, Eibhlín and myself would go to the chapel to see the crib. 'Don't stay there long!' she said.

I caught the children by the hands and off we went. The night was dark but indeed you could pick out the tiniest object on the pavement by the light of all the candles in the windows. When we entered the chapel, praise be to God! it was a beautiful sight with lamps lighting and the altar decorated with a mass of candles all ablaze. The crib was at the side of the altar and if you were the dullest person who ever lived it would remind you of the Kingdom of Heaven. The nuns were playing sweet hymns and my heart was filled with joy and pleasure as I listened to music the likes of which I had never heard before.

I scrutinized everything around me so that I didn't find the time passing. I got a start when I heard the thump of Séamaisín's head hitting the altar rail; the poor little man was falling asleep.

'Let's go home, darling,' I said, 'you're sleepy.'

It was ten o'clock when we arrived home.

'Sit down here now,' Nell said, 'I have boiled milk and sweet cake for ye.'

She didn't put me in a place where I'd feel humbled and I had my share as well as the rest. Before we were ready Seáinín and his father came in after having been out for a stroll.

'*Sha,* let's go on our knees in the name of God and say the rosary,' Nan said.

When we were finished: 'Off to sleep with ye now, my little clan,' Séamas said.

There was no need for him to say it a second time. They went upstairs to bed. I remained on with Nell and Séamas in the kitchen until twelve o'clock and we had a great deal of chat and pleasant company. I recited 'The Welcome of the Child Jesus,' for them. This is how I began it:

Seventeen hundred thousand welcomes
Nine and twenty times and more
To the Son of the God of Glory
Whom the Virgin Mary bore,
Who to her glorious womb descended
In His essence, God and man,
For upon the Eve of Christmas
The King of Kings his reign began.

And on the eighth day thereafter,
Circumcision Feast its name,
In the Temple of the Triune
His precious blood when shed, became
Clearest portent for the faithful
That for Him the future chill
Held a bitter grievous passion
And a Cross on Calvary's Hill.

Hail to thee, most Glorious Virgin
Queen of Heaven without a taint
Who, entering life as white as angel
Was baptized as pure as saint.
Never, never, sin committed,
Neither knew its track nor trace
From whose womb emerged in triumph
Christ who saved the human race.

Hail once more, the glorious Virgin
Maiden powerful, mild and good
Beating her two palms together
As her tears were changed to blood.
As the heavens darkened o'er her
And the sun refused to shine
God's Son on the Cross spreadeagled
Who had ne'er committed crime.

The Son of the God of Glory
Is my treasure beyond all
And my heart and restless spirit
Make no marvel at His call,

For 'twas He in crucifixion
On the rood His blood had shed—
The poisoned lance it pierced His heartstrings
And the Crown of Thorns His Head.

Then the rabble black as midnight
Bore Christ to His burial place,
Not a board to clothe His body
Nor cloak of silk to shield His face
And the smooth flesh of the Saviour
Was laid low in yellow clay
And the mighty stone upended
To await the Judgement Day.

He shall hold that same appearance
Till the heavens are rent in twain,
Till the sepulchres are opened
And the dead shall rise again,
Till the trumpet-blast is sounded
At the dawnlight's primal ray—
From the Hill the King will listen
On that awful Judgement Day.

Christians of this troubled world
Make your peace with God above
Cry your sins in full contrition
Beat your breasts in sorrowed love.
Scorn to sell your bright Redeemer
For gleaming gold or wealth that dies
For this life is but a plaything
When compared with Paradise.

When the poem was ended Séamas put his hand into his pocket and handed me a half-crown.

'Here!' he said, 'a little Christmas box for you.'

I took it; needless to say I was pleased.

'You'll have to teach me that hymn, Margaret,' he said.

'I will and welcome, Master,' I told him and I meant what I said.

'Bedtime now in God's name!' Nell said. 'We'll be getting up early in the morning for Mass.'

Then we went to bed.

Shrovetide Doings

*How Máire Bheag's match was made — Micky and his
capers — Poor Micky is laid low by 'The Laddo from Cork'
— Micky turns his back on drink from that out!*

SATURDAY came and with it came the Shrovetide Fair.
There was a great throng of people in Dingle on that day
—this despite the fact the weather was wet and sloppy
and that the rain was slashing down. I was half-idle
because the fair wasn't yet over, so I was standing in the
doorway watching the people.

'Bless my soul,' I told myself, 'it's no harm to say that
people are real fidgety during Shrove!' And that's no
wonder because many's the one of them has a fine fat
purse stored away in the hopes of marrying his daughter
into a farm of land. And many's the person too puts it
together carefully and miserly and then pitches it into a
place where, as the saying goes, even the unborn calf is
eaten!'

On the other side of the street I saw three men and two
women having a confidential chat. I knew them well for
they were customers of the man of the house. Their hair
was drenched with rain and eventually they had to run
for it; they made straight across the street to our house
and when they arrived at the door, 'You're wet, Micky!'
I said.

'Blast it, girl, I'm drenched,' Micky said pushing in
past me; the others followed.

Peaid Thomáisín, his wife and Micky came first; three
or four more followed. They were all standing at the
counter for a while and Séamas came out from the
kitchen to greet them.

'Bless ye, men! There ye are!' he said.

'The same to you!' said Peaid Thomáisín.

84

'I'd take my oath that ye have some business on hands,' Séamas said again.

'We have indeed,' said Peaid. 'We're fixing up a match this day, my decent man!'

'You'll shake up the old purse so?' said Séamas.

'I'm a fair while putting it together!' said Peaid. 'There's no one for it but Máire Bheag.'

'Good luck to ye!' Séamas said. 'Who's the man?'

'Seán Bheit, a good boy, God bless him!' said Peaid.

'You may rest assured that he is good,' said Séamas. 'A quiet, sensible, well-thought-of lad. Where are the rest —or did Micilín come?'

'He didn't, for he wasn't well. But a man every bit as good as him came—Micky here—a man with a generous heart.'

'He's good!' said Séamas. 'Ye'd be better off sitting below in the room. I own to God but today will be a great day for making matches, because everyone will be inside out of the rain.'

They were hardly seated when Máire Bheag, her mother, and two more young women arrived and they faced down for where the others were. I assure you that they got a fine welcome. Nothing would satisfy them but to have Máire Bheag sit down beside the young man. Seán was a grand, handsome boy and any young woman would only be too delighted to take a seat beside him.

Before long the table got a rattle. 'Go on down, Margaret,' Nell told me.

As soon as I went down, Peaid let this yell out of him: 'Bring me down a can of porter, girl!'

I brought down the porter and handed the vessel to Peaid. He filled out the first measure for Micky. Micky took a powerful swig of the drink but then he shook his head and put a scowl on his face.

'This stuff would perish Ould Nick himself this day,' he said. 'I'd rather one mouthful of the hot stuff than what's in the house of this porter.'

'Right you are!' said Siobhán. 'I'd prefer it myself, too!'

'The girls'll take a small drop of punch to warm them up. Bring me up a pint of whiskey!'

I brought it up and set it on the table for him.

'Ha-ha! That's the boyo!' he said.

'Watch out, Micky,' I said, referring to the whiskey, 'or "the laddo from Cork" will outfox you!'

'Not at all, girl! Often he tried to put one across me, but just the same, we'll knock today out of him—'tisn't often we get it!'

He began to dole out the drink among those present. Speaking to myself, Siobhán said: 'Bring me out a drop of hot water and a fist of sugar.'

I did so and I can tell you that it didn't take Siobhán long to make the punch and serve it out to the girls. Bríghde, the mother of the young woman, took a fair amount too.

I had to leave them then because I got a call to another part of the premises; on days like that I was very busy— but when I'd get the chance I'd pay Micky a visit. Micky was a hearty fellow and a first-class man in company, too.

On one of the occasions that I went down to them they were fine and merry and they had no shortage of speech. Micky was in great tongue, piping up with *An Gamhain Geal Bán*—'The Bright White Calf'—and Bríghde and Siobhán were in such trim that you'd think they'd kiss the mouths off each other. Such flattery and fine speeches! Peaid Thomáis had a grip of the young man's hand and he was speechifying away with big rocks of words, saying that he was the man able to satisfy him as regards the money question, and saying too that he hoped that himself and Máire Bheag would be lucky. Then Seán turned to the young woman, put his arm around her waist and started to sing:

> *And my woman I'd prefer*
> *And my woman I'd prefer*
> *Than top or tail of her dowry-o.*

The match was made, the day was getting late and they certainly had enough drank. Micky had more than his share consumed. I told Séamas that I'd have to go for the cow.

''Tis time!' he said, 'because the early part of the night will be very dark.'

He went down into the taproom. ' 'Twill make a right dark night,' he said. 'Better for ye be going home.'

'Right, Séamas,' said Bríghde. 'We have a long road before us.'

Then they began to leave the taproom: I threw my headshawl across my shoulders and went off for the cow.

By the time I returned to the house with the cow it was very dark. I opened the door of the back garden and let her go off down in front of me. I had to go back through the kitchen because the door of the cow-house was closed from the inside—this because horses were stabled in it sometimes. When I took the bolt off the door to let in the cow I realized that there was a big bulk stretched out on the ground outside the door. I bent down to examine it but I wasn't clear what it was. I placed my hand on it and then I realized it was a body. In I went, fit to drop life!

'God, Séamas!' I said, 'there's a dead man stretched in the doorway of the cow-house and I can't put the cow in.'

'A dead man?' he said and he got a right fright.

He took a candle and a box of matches: he lit the candle but he couldn't recognize who was there because the man's mouth and face were turned downwards and he was stretched out like a dead log across the threshold.

'I don't know from God, who he is,' Séamas said, 'but no matter who he is, he's finished.'

Nell arrived. 'God save us!' she said, 'this never happened as long as I've been in the house.'

'Take hold of the candle to see would we be able to lift him into the kitchen,' Séamas said.

The poor woman was trembling all over with fright: I was no great shakes myself and indeed we weren't a whole lot of help to Séamas at that time.

'Margaret, you grip him with me,' Séamas said.

Even so we couldn't shift him one bit! Just then Seáinín arrived and gave us a hand; we succeeded in turning the man in such a way that we got a look at his face.

'Uh-oh,' says Seáinín, 'it's Micky!'

'Micky it is!' said Séamas. 'Isn't he a great loss?'

'Maybe he isn't dead at all, Dad,' Seánín said. 'If we could only bring him into the kitchen . . .'

'I'm afraid he's as dead as a door-nail,' Séamas said. 'It's a great pity and we'll be blamed for his death. But that makes no matter, we've only to do our best first.'

We dragged him with us; he was as stiff as a poker and we were tugging away with him until we got him in. Nell arranged sacks in the corner and we stretched him out down on top of them.

'If his boots were taken off.' she said, 'and his feet placed in hot water . . .'

I took off his boots and got a vessel of hot water and began massaging his feet in it. Séamas had a cup of whiskey and he was rubbing the spirits to his mouth and to the palms of his hands when Nan walked in.

'*Aililiú!*' she said. 'What's goin' on here? It's no good for ye to be at him, but if there's a spark left in his heart there's nothing better than melted butter—if it could be got back his throat. If it's drink he has taken he'll vomit it out then—that's if he's alive at all.'

Nell got the butter and started putting it into his mouth with a spoon but alas! his teeth were locked together.

'If the handle of the spoon was forced between his teeth, maybe you could pour it back,' Nan said.

Séamas got the handle of the spoon and put it between Micky's teeth and Nell succeeded in pouring the butter back his throat.

'No mercy! Give him plenty of it,' Nan said.

She was right; after a quarter of an hour Micky started to vomit.

'Thanks be to God he's alive,' Nell said, 'and he won't be a ha'porth the worse for it.' I assure you that Micky got attention if anybody ever got it!

'What about the priest?' Nell asked.

'We won't bother with either priest or doctor,' Séamas said. 'He doesn't need them, because from the minute he starts vomiting the drink, straightaway he'll be as good as ever. No one will know; otherwise the whole country-side will go wild with the news.'

It was nearly twelve o'clock by the time Micky had the proper use of himself. When he came to his senses he didn't know where he was nor what had happened to him. Séamas told him where he had been lying and said that if it weren't for me and the white cow no one would know where he was until morning.

'But you have escaped with your life now, thank God,' Séamas said, 'and you should have sense from this out.'

'It wasn't the drink altogether that did for me,' said Micky, 'but that blasted pipe—I smoked too much of it. I remember going to the back garden but I remember no more.'

'Drink a drop of tea and you'll be as good as ever,' Nell told him.

I set the tea aside to draw and everyone of us drank a cup. The night was ruined on us, but now that Micky was out of his predicament we were all delighted, especially Séamas, because I daresay it could have more serious consequences for him than for anyone else.

''Twill be a long day, Micky,' I said, 'before you'll drink as much as you did.'

'You can bet your life on that, girl,' Micky said.

'Don't say it!' Séamas said, joking him.

'I say it and I mean it,' the other fellow said. 'As sure as my name is Micky not a drop o' drink will enter my mouth again as long as I live.' We began to poke fun at him.

'I swear to ye that I'm not joking,' he said, 'I'd swear by the black curses that Finn put on the *báirneachs** that

*One fine autumn afternoon Fionn Mac Cumhail was on a grassy plot on the edge of Ventry Harbour. The sea was calm and the tide was fully ebbed. Fionn got a mind for a roast of *báirneachs* or limpets. He went out to where the *báirneachs* were on the stones and gathered a small quantity of them. He made a fire of wood which was plentiful about him at that time and when the fire was red he set the *báirneachs* to roast. He noticed nothing until a king-warrior who had come ashore unknown to him, addressed him. Fionn was startled; he was ashamed of the fact that he was roasting *báirneachs,* but he made some excuse to the warrior and said that he was a cowherd employed by the Fianna and that Fionn Mac Cumhail and his men were in the castle above—the one we call Rahinnane (or Rathconane). Then the warrior moved off towards the castle. As soon as Fionn found that he had gone, 'Indeed,' he said, 'I swear by the black curses that never again will the King of the Fianna know such shame!' And the Irish have that as a byword ever since—'I swear by the black curses—what Fionn swore on the *báirneachs!*'

I'll never again touch a drop of drink the longest day I live.

He kept that promise, because never again did a drop pass his lips from that until the day he died.

'As well for you stay where you are till morning,' Séamas said.

'I'll belt away towards the latter end of the night,' said Micky, 'and I'll be on my road home before anyone sees me. I suppose Cáit is out of her mind thinking that I'm lying dead in some ditch.'

'You went close enough to it,' Séamas said.

'I did so, boy. But I won't go again with God's help. But whisper, Nell.' he added, 'for the Lord's sake let none of ye tell Cáit what happened me because she'd sweep the head off me.'

'Don't be a bit afraid of that," said Nell. 'There's no fear anyone will hear about it.'

He settled himself nicely in the corner and before long he was snoring.

'Ye might as well go to bed,' Nan said. 'Margaret and myself will stay in the kitchen till he goes home.'

They bade us good-night and with the exception of Nan and myself they all went to sleep. It was then about three o'clock and Nan was dozing away in the chair. I was seated in front of the fire resting my cheek on the palm of my hand and I was going over things in my mind. There was no sound to be heard except a snore from Micky and the tick-tock of the clock. A kind of mysterious loneliness came over me, but just the same I was thinking of Máire Bheag—that she was sleeping fine and comfortable at that moment—that is, if she hadn't a nightmare that Seán Bheit had run off with another girl! What would she do if that happened and all the love she had for him! I thought that the world was queer, to tie a fine boy like him to a tawny little lump like her—but then indeed three hundred pounds gave her a fine complexion!

Seán could have got many a fine girl to marry him but that wouldn't do his people at all for it wasn't a fine woman they wanted but money. Often Bríghde would say with a snort of disgust that beauty didn't boil the pot!

The old people cared for nothing but their own satisfaction even if that meant having the son troubled in his
mind and tied to a good-for-nothing slattern for the rest
of his days. There's an old saying that 'Pounds vanish
but pouts remain!' and that same might be said for Seán
Bheit because it doesn't take long to spend a dowry and
all he'd have afterwards was Máire Bheag. I don't think
that he ever again had peace of mind after that day.

About five o'clock Micky woke up. 'I'll be shortening
my road. In all that ever happened me I'd rather be home
before anyone would spot me.'

'It's all the damn same to you, Micky,' I told him, 'when the "laddo from Cork" didn't despatch you to the other world. Didn't you always hear it said that a good man is still good the day after he has been drunk.'

'Girl, you're dead right! That laddo will never again get a chance at me for the rest of my days. Good luck to ye now!'

'Good luck to you too,' said Nan, 'and every thanks go to God that you didn't meet your doom in our place.'

I locked the door after him and Nan and myself went to bed. I never knew a thing until it was eight o'clock the next day.

The following Tuesday morning there was a number of weddings in Ballyferriter; Máire Bheag and Seán were there and they were the first couple to be married. There was a large crowd of people at the wedding breakfast. Séamas and Seáinín were there with everybody else and when Séamas arrived home the following morning I questioned him about the wedding. Anyway I asked him how things went with Micky or was he drunk.

'Devil a drunk!' said Séamas. 'Not a drop went past his lips and this surprised a number of people.'

'They wouldn't be a bit surprised,' I said, 'if they knew what happened last Saturday night.'

'Right!' said Séamas. 'But I don't think anything like that will happen him again.'

'I suppose Máire Bheag was cocked up to the height of vanity with the fine man she got,' I asked.

'No wonder she would,' Séamas said. 'There wasn't as fine a young man as him in Ballyferriter yesterday, God bless him. It's a good job that Máire Bheag's father had the purse to back her; only for he had she wouldn't have had Seán, for many a lovely girl had her eye on him.'

'If he didn't marry her she'd have died the death for the love of him!' I said.

'She'd go a fair way towards that same, child,' Nell said, 'for you can't beat love. Did you hear what the man said:

92

May plague and colic love devour
For woe to him who's in its power,
Love has left me sick and sore
And healing I shall know no more.

'I'll go to bed and leave ye at it,' Séamas said.

Seáinín and himself went off to bed and badly they needed it for they were disturbed after events of the night.

Exciting Stories in Dingle

The tale of Muiris O'Shea and the landlord's bullocks — A brave woman protecting her husband — The welcome for Brighdín of John Street

'THERE'S hope from a prison but none from the grave.' The proverb, I suppose, is true, for anyone who enters the grave has no possible chance of getting out. Often when I'd be weary and worn out from the world I'd begin to think that I'd be better off dead than alive but, of course, these things never come to pass.

I often told Nan that she had a fine life; her answer was, 'Have patience, girl. Whatever is in store for you, you'll get it.'

'There's nothing in store for me, Nan, except poverty and heartbreak forever.'

'You imagine, girl, when you see people with means, that they live contented lives. Don't be one bit jealous of them! They have their own share of the troubles of the world.'

'I'd say, Nan,' I said, 'that you have no idea what it means to be like me.'

'Too well I know it!' Nan said, 'for when I was your age I hadn't a bite to eat nor a mouthful to drink. That's the time, child, that the people were in hunger and want. I remember well that it's many a long day I gave working for other people and all I'd earn was a small scrap of food. As far as my judgement goes they had no option: the bad times were there and the people hadn't food for themselves.'

'Do you remember Muiris O'Shea?' I asked her.

'I remember him well,' she said. 'I was a right plump little lassie at that time. That poor man got sincere

94

prayers from the people because many's the one got a juicy morsel because of what he did.'

'I suppose he was guilty!'

'Oyeh, probably he was among the men who did it,' Nan went on. 'He'd have got away with it too, only for the scoundrel who hopped over on the side of the law and gave the game away—aye, and himself as guilty as anyone! Whatever cattle the old Lord owned were down on their rumps after the night for every single one of them had its houghs slashed.'

'Why was that done, Nan?'

'The boys wanted to get their own back on the landlord because five tenants, close relatives of their own, had been evicted without mercy, and they wanted some satisfaction out of him. That's why they cut the houghs of all the cattle.'

'Ye had plenty meat at that time?'

'Indeed it relieved many a starving poor devil of the hunger. At that time my house was only a hundred yards from Muiris's house and I remember well when he escaped from Bunatrohane Bridge out by the side of the bay to Reenbeg. The poor fellow was arrested in his bed and they were bringing him to Ballygoleen. One of the men who was handcuffed to him had no sight in one eye. Muiris pretended that he wanted to make some delay; when he found himself ready to go he drew a belt of his fist across the constable's good eye and knocked him flat on his back. Off he raced and when he reached Reenbeg he started swimming across the mouth of the bay. He succeeded in reaching the strand on the other side and away with him then and trace nor tidings of him they never found until such time as the old Lord of Bally-goleen and his wife were buried; the day following the Lady's burial Muiris O'Shea was back again in Dingle. While he was away from home he composed the verses.'

'Was it how he was lonely because of being away from his wife and home?'

'Likely so, child. People had a habit at that time of composing poetry whenever loneliness came over them —this so as to banish the sorrow from their hearts.'

'Do you know the poem, Nan?'

'Would I doubt you, child! I haven't it too accurately. Maybe you'ld like to hear it?'

'Be sure I would,' I said. Then she began to recite:

> One quiet pleasant morning
> As on my couch I slept
> Yellow George and his minions
> Surrounded me like theft;
> With cruel bonds a prisoner
> They bound me without warning
> In Ballygoleen they dallied
> Drinking wine till morning.
>
> And as the day was breaking
> Speckling the eastern sky,
> Carefully I noted
> The peeler standing by.
> Blind Foran then I hammered
> In his left eye and felled him,
> Hugging the cliffside trouserless
> To Reenbeg I skeltered.
>
> Jesus knows right well
> As does the True King of Angels,
> That 'twasn't for the sake of luscious beef
> I learned the trade of maiming,
> But to lead the broken Irish
> Destroyed on many occasions,
> For which I suffered sorely
> And lost my loved locations.
>
> My curse on my companions,
> On each father and each mother,
> Who let me into banishment,
> Without a single brother
> Who failed to murder Graddy
> On a night was dark or pale,
> But 'twas he that paid the reckoning
> With his nine months in jail.

Here at the Rock of Patrick
Is my choice of Ireland's women
To whom I gave allegiance
And was part of woe's dominion;
For Lena is broken-hearted
Begging the neighbours' bounty.
I drink her health a score of times
Alone in Ely country.

Oh, I'm sore tormented
Since I abandoned home,
My children gone awandering
Their mother all alone.
But I'll return again
When Her Ladyship is clay;
And through Dingle Town in triumph
Shall walk Muiris Mór O'Shea.

'I'd say his wife was lonely after him, Nan?'

'She was, girl, but what could she do?' Nan said. Then: 'Have *you* anything to do at this time of day?'

'I have indeed, Nan, and a great deal to do. But I'm very interested in stories like that.'

I went out, taking the brush with me, and began sweeping out the hall. When I put my head outside the door I saw a man coming up the street. He had a mule and a common cart: his head was sunk on his breast and you'd know that he had a drop of drink taken. There was a woman with him—a powerful closely-set mallet of a dame. He stopped the mule at the kerb and came into the shop. Muiris Shéamais Mhicil was this man's name and he was a poor labourer with no means except his day's hire.

'You didn't go home yet, Muiris?' I asked him.

'It's early yet, girl!' he replied.

Cáit, his wife, came in after him and the boss of the house was chatting with them for a while. Then Cáit moved off to the back part of the house, and in she goes to the turf-house, a fine dark hole under the stairs where we kept the turf.

I went in after her; she called to me in a low voice: 'Bring me in a glass of whiskey and don't let Muiris know that I'm here.' I brought her the glass.

'Now darling, bring me in a fistful of matches.'

'By the heavens above, but you've notions, my lassie,' I said in my own mind. I brought her the matches and before long she was fogging smoke out of a big white clay pipe.

'Is Muiris outside yet?' she asked in a half-whisper.

'They're still talking,' I said.

She called for a second glass; I brought it to her and she poured it back her throat. She was on her grug there all the while puffing away at the old pipe. Whatever glance I gave towards the door, I saw a man coming in— a huge long legger of a countryman wearing a fine suit of clothes and you could nearly have shaved yourself in the gloss he had in his boots! He moved up close beside Muiris.

'You're the very man I wanted,' he said.

'Why so?' Muiris asked.

'Because you won't leave this spot without the taste of blood on your teeth.' You'd know the man was angry by the way he spoke.

'To tell the truth, my decent man,' Muiris said, 'you're picking the wrong man in me for trying out your strength.'

'Right!' said Séamas putting his head in between them, because he wanted to make peace. But the other fellow was spoiling for a row and he kept at Muiris in loud, angry tones.

'Who's that talking?' Cáit asked me; I was standing in the doorway.

'I don't know him from a crow, Cáit,' I told her. 'But he's a big able man and he's talking threateningly to Muiris.'

She stuck her head out of the turf-hole and gave a squint at the big fellow. She knew well who he was!

'Bad luck may melt him, child! He's an ould enemy of Muiris's!'

She gathered her shawl around her two shoulders and broke off the stem of the pipe she had in her mouth. She

98

squeezed her fist around the pipe-head and off out she goes to the big fellow. King Billy never had a soldier as brave as she was at that particular moment; she stood straight in front of the huge man.

'What the hell picking have you on that poor man every day of the week?' she asked him.

'He'll know before he leaves where he is,' the big fellow answered.

'You'll strike him, is it?'

'Strike him I will and belt the lard out of him too.'

With that Cáit hits him above the eyes with the pipe-head she had in her hand and lifts him clear and clean off the ground. He falls head first against the counter.

'There you are, you devil! Who's atin' the clay now?' she asked. 'Mop up that!' she said then, for a stream of blood was flowing down the big fellow's cheek.

'God strengthen your hand!' Séamas said. 'It's a good job for Muiris that he has you to back him.'

'A good job for him too, that when he married a woman at all 'twasn't a foolah he married,' she said.

Muiris was only a simpleton; he was too easy-going and everyone was down on top of him.

The big fellow came to his feet and he remained as quiet as a child while Nell was washing the blood off him.

'Someone'll pay for the dirty treatment I got,' he said.

'Big wind, I declare,' Cáit said. Then: 'Séamas, put out a half-sack of flour and we'll be going home. That big fellah there is no joke at all!'

The flour was put on the cart and Séamas stood herself and Muiris a drink.

'Drink that, Cáit,' he said. 'You did a deed today that I never saw a woman doing before.'

'You can take it from me, neighbour,' said Cáit, 'that Muiris's skull would have been in porridge long ago if he hadn't me there to back him. Look at the big fellow now as quiet as a ewe lamb. He can be putting sticking plaster on himself now!'

When they had the drink taken they went off out the door. Muiris sat on one side of the cart, Cáit sat on the other and they headed for home.

The big fellow had nothing better to do than to clean himself as best he could. There wasn't a word out of him now. What had he to say? There was his eyebrow hanging loose after Cáit and her chalk sword! He slipped out the door.

''Pon my soul,' said Séamas, 'your man going out isn't too thankful for his bargain.'

'He'll be ashamed, I'll bet,' said Nell, 'especially since it was a woman slashed him.'

Just then Seáinín rushed in, in a state of great excitement.

'Easy, boy,' I said. 'What's wrong with you?'

'Bríghdín of John Street is coming home tonight,' he said in great glee.

'Tonight?'—this from Séamas.

'Aye, and there'll be bonfires at the Little Bridge and candles lighting in every window to make "illuminations" for her. We'll have them too, Margaret!' And off he romped giving every hop-skip-and-jump with delight.

'Who's Bríghdín?' I asked Séamas, because I knew nothing about her.

'Bríghdín Kennedy, a poor girl from the top of John Street. She has been in jail for six months but her term is up now.'

'God protect us! What did she do out of the way that they put her in jail?'

'Not a thing!' said Séamas, 'and it's a great pity that everyone isn't as true as her. She knew secretly the people who stole the peeler's horse out of the barracks here one night; the authorities wanted that information badly and the police tried by every possible means to get the information from her but they failed. They promised her three hundred pounds if she'd tell them; the answer she gave was that her secret was her own affair and that she'd prefer to die rather than have it thrown in her face that she was cowardly, or that she'd reveal what was in her mind. The poor girl was clapped into jail where she has served six months with hard labour. There you have it now,' Séamas went on, 'and it's no wonder that there'll be a great welcome for her tonight.'

It was now supper-time; everyone was hurrying to have the tea over so as to be ready for the band when it'd move out.

We had the tea just finished when we heard the band in full blast at the top of the town. Everyone raced out. I turned to Nell and said in a wheedling tone of voice, 'Can I follow the band?'

I hadn't much confidence that she'd allow me, for as a general rule, she wouldn't let me out at night.

'Take Eibhlín and Séamas with you,' she said. 'The weather is fine but watch them very carefully.'

'I'll do that, with God's help,' I said. My soul! I wouldn't have chosen going to heaven at that moment!

As soon as we were outside the door the band came down the street towards us. There was a crowd of strapping young men in the band at that time and they were playing 'O'Donnell Abú.' When they went down the street there was a bonfire at the Little Bridge and there were bonfires in other places as well. Twice the band did the round of the town; every possible window was illuminated with lighting candles—all except the homes of the loyalists and their windows were pitch dark. But no matter how carefully the peelers kept guard, those windows were in smithereens by morning!

When the band had returned to its headquarters myself and my tiny pair went home safely; we had the rest of the night in which to thresh out the events of the day—this until it was time to go to bed.

More Adventures

'Baby' Gray — A street fight with the police — How we almost drowned the cow in the swamp

THAT was how my days passed in that happy house. One year, two years, and a third year passed by to my satisfaction in their company. At the end of that time I found some little thing amiss with my health. I wasn't as well as I'd like to be nor was I as strong as was necessary to do my work. From day to day I thought that the trouble would pass and that there would be no need for me to take a rest. But things never turn out as one anticipates.

Early one morning in the beginning of May I was sound asleep when Séamas called me. It was the morning of a fair-day and he had cattle to take to the fair, so I had to get up very early to prepare the breakfast. I hopped out of bed although the megrims of sleep were still going round in my head—but that was no time for dawdling. I kindled the fire; the turf was dry—we used no coal—and the breakfast was prepared before Séamas was ready. Then himself and Seáinín went off with the cattle.

It was still very early and I hadn't much to do so I stood in the doorway that looked out on the street. It was a pleasant time of day and there wasn't a puff of wind in the sky. The sun was rising above the town. I heard no sound but the chatter of rooks among the trees to the west of me. At that moment I could see nothing but the great long street that stretched from John Street to the Holy Stone. The sun was shining on the windows and one would think that the panes of glass were reflecting flames of fire. As yet there weren't many people on the street; neither was there sound nor cry except when now and again a man, or two men, moved past me driving a bunch of cattle to the fair.

I remained standing in the doorway. My thoughts were getting out of hand. 'Life is strange,' I said in my own mind. 'Here are shopkeepers all set to turn a shilling and here too are country-people with their hearts and their health broken trying to earn those same shillings and when they have them they proceed to throw them to the shopkeepers in the evening!'

I was thinking too of what the future held in store for myself. I had come to the house as a child but I was now a young woman of seventeen years of age so that the days of my childhood were over and a new life lay before me. Three and a half years had passed since I left home and I hadn't laid eyes on it nor on my poor sorrowing mother since then. It was a long span indeed, but just the same I was only a little child when I left it. Now I was a bouncer of a young woman! Wouldn't she be delighted if I walked in the door to her! But the worst part of the story was my having to go back to her without my health being up to the mark. I wasn't feeling as strong as I ought to be, and I was convinced that I would have to give up the work. My thoughts were rambling on and on as to how I'd have to return home in poor health—the home that I had to leave when I was young because my presence on its floor was begrudged.

No cure for it now! Every sign read that I'd have to go back. I drew a sigh and I never knew a thing in the wide world until Nell called me. I turned. 'One would think you're dreaming,' she said.

'I wasn't far from it, I assure you,' I answered.

'Bring up a can of water,' she said, 'for you won't have time to draw it until daylight again.' I grabbed the can and went off for the water. There was plenty of country-people on the street at that hour; one man had cattle, another sheep, a third potatoes and each and every one of them had his own interest to look after. What with the scurrying, the noise and the to-and-fro-ing, the street was not quiet by now! Before long Séamas came along with a bunch of cattle and they were driven west to the yard. His dinner had to be got ready. Seáinín was as hungry as a ploughman; he begrudged even one moment's delay for he was ravenous after the morning.

103

'Was it a good fair today?' Nell asked. 'Did ye sell the cattle?'

'I sold some and bought more,' Séamas answered. 'They'll have to be left where they are until evening when the people will scatter. There are as many people in the town today as would make war on the British Crown!'

When it was ready he and Seáinín sat down to the dinner.

I left them there and went out, for I always made a trip to the door whenever I got the chance. I wasn't long standing there when I saw the people moving in a haphazard kind of way and running up towards Muiris Bán's house. There was a kind of uproar and grappling going on and by this time so many people had gathered that if a pin dropped from the sky it'd fall right down on top of someone's head. Before long I saw a pair of policemen in battle-dress coming down the street and moving at a right gait-of-go; each man had a helmet on his head with a spike the length of the leg of a tongs sticking out of the top of it. Their teeth were clenched and they were breathing heavily through their nostrils with the dint of the pace at which they moved. Two others moved behind them and again two more—all moving at the same speed.

The first pair pushed through the crowd. God help your head! it was little use for them to do so! The people fighting were right wicked and they were talking in loud angry tones. Meanwhile, the policemen were trying—unsuccessfully—to force their way through the throng. 'The devil,' I told myself, 'this is a proper pitched battle!'

In I went to the kitchen in a state of great agitation.

'What's wrong with you?' Séamas asked.

'Man alive!' I said, 'there has never been such a set-to since the time of the Dingle slaughter as is now going on at Muirisín Bán's house. All the peelers from Tralee to Dingle are there and they're making no hand of it at all!'

'Dead right, they aren't,' Séamas said, 'for that disturbance is only an excuse to draw the peelers to the scene. Some of the country-people have no gentle feelings for police and indeed, bad right for them if they had, for the peelers pitched a poor penniless woman and her five orphans out of her home a few days ago. I heard that her brother swore an oath that day that before God he hoped to get the chance of vengeance—above board or underhand.' And then Séamas went on, 'I pity the man that'd stand in the path of his blows for he's a wild man and he's black out against them.'

'I own to God!' I said, 'there's a good block of a stout yellow brute trying to force his way through the crowd but he's making no headway.'

'That's the worst scoundrel that ever stood in Dingle.' Séamas said. 'No one has a good word to say for him!'

As soon as he had his dinner eaten Séamas went off out the door. I went upstairs and stuck my head out the window at a point where I had a splendid view. They were still at the lambasting; the screeching and commotion were going strong. I saw the police charging in and grabbing the big man by the hand. Straightaway another policeman drew a blow of his fist and struck the big man across the bridge of the nose.

'Let me go!' the big fellow told the peeler, 'or I'll smash your ugly mouth!'

The words were scarcely out of his mouth when, with his left hand clenched, he let fly into the peeler's teeth, lifted him into the air and stretched him on the flat of his back in the channel. But if he did, the peeler held on to him with a vice-like grip and brought the big man with him to the ground. Now there was uproar and hullabaloo! Like a flash, the big fellow was on the top of the peeler and believe you me, he didn't spare him but vented the full force of his rage on him. More peelers crashed in and one of them got a puck here and another got a push there. One of the crowd would stretch out his leg in front of a policeman so as to trip him up, and another, meeting a peeler as he whirled round, would give him a belt in the poll and send his cap flying to the street. The police were now being hammered and clattered until word reached the barracks that there was a wicked fight in progress. The D.I. didn't take long to get ready.

He came east towards the Little Bridge riding on a black gelding that had a white blaze on its forehead. When he reached the Little Bridge he blew on a bugle and as he did so the roaring broke out from the mass of people above. I looked in the direction of the Little Bridge; the D.I. had travelled some distance up the street by this time. He was a brave young man all accoutred, carrying his weapons, and riding on the black gelding. He had vigour and ferocity in his eyes and he boded no good for the crowd at the top of the town. He had a long wicked-looking spear in front of his horse and, judging by the jingling and noise of the harness bells on the animal, you'd think he was Ould Nick himself. He moved past me up the street and I assure you that his intentions seemed anything but wholesome! He blew a second blast on his bugle and, God of Miracles! the people scattered before him like small birds. Within five minutes there wasn't a solitary Christian on the street except three men who had been engaged in the fighting and who had been arrested by the police. The rider went up and down the street twice and 'twould be a brave man who wouldn't quail before him. The horse was as well trained as its rider. And if it was your very last laugh you'd have to laugh that day, for one policeman was missing his cap and another man had his ribs smashed and the sallow-complexioned fellow was cut to ribbons and in a sorry state. All in all the people weren't too thankful for their bargain.

When peace was restored I asked Séamas who the horseman was.

' "Baby" Gray, the D.I.,' he said.

I saw him often after this. I knew his face well and I recalled this day of disturbance when I heard that 'Baby' Gray and his followers had fallen at the hands of Tomás Ashe at Ashbourne.

As everything had cooled off by this time, and the street was clear of people, Séamas said that it would be better to drive the cattle to Kilfountan for he generally grazed them there. Needless to say, myself and Seáinín were delighted. The cattle were driven out. We went up Goat Street with the beasts moving ahead of us and everything was going smack-smooth until we came within a hundred yards of the gateway that the cattle were to enter; then the devil picked one of them and she gave a buck-jump across the fence. But she didn't succeed in clearing the obstacle for there was a deep grype of water inside the fence and down she goes! All we could see of her was her head and the point of her rump. Dear God, we were in a terrible fix! The beast was done for and not a person within a mile's radius of us to rescue her.

'Is she drowned?' Seáinín asked.

'She is, boy,' I said, 'and that she may be drowned and battered! It's an old saying that if you stick yourself into a hole you deserve to stay in it! This one here has landed herself in a hole that she'll stay in!'

We were there on top of the fence with no idea what best to do.

'My father'll slaughter us, Margaret!'

'Slaughter us he will!' I replied. Then: 'Seldom with this road to be as deserted as it is.'

'The fighting terrified the people,' Seáinín said. 'They're all gone away home.' He was whingeing crying.

'Don't be a bit in dread, lad,' I told him. 'God's help is nearer than the door.'

Whatever look I gave around me what should I see coming up Milltown Height but a horse and cart.

'There's a horse coming, Seáinín,' I said, 'and there might be someone in the car who'd rescue the animal.'

'She's dead now, I'd say,' Seáinín replied.

'She's not, sonny. She's still shaking her ears.'

The horse was drawing nearer and moving at a lively pace.

'God's help to us,' I said, and I was delighted. 'It's Donncha Mhicíl's horse and there are three men in the car.'

When they had come abreast of us, Mícheál Óg, for he was driving the horse, spoke up. 'Save my soul! What brought ye here?'

'Whatever brought us here,' I said, 'we're in trouble, for one of the beasts jumped across the fence and I suppose she's drowned.'

Three of them jumped out of the car immediately and Mícheál Óg took the winkers and reins off the horse. He gave a wild jump from the top of the fence and got his footing on a green tuft of grass growing on the other side of the grype. Then he tied one end of the reins around the cow's horns and the other end around her rump. The other two men caught hold of the rope midways and dragged her up. It didn't take them long to do so for they braced their feet against the ditch and gave her one pull that brought her clear and clean over the top of the fence.

'God leave ye yeer strength!' I said when I saw they had the beast out on the road. But, man dear, she looked like a small shaved drowned rat. And she was barely able to put her legs under her.

'My solemn oath,' I said to Ciotóg, one of the three men, 'if she had "gandy" in her while ago she has very little of it left now.'

They began rubbing her and walking her and before long she was able to walk well. They headed her off for us in the direction of the other cattle. Mícheál Óg opened the gate and we left them in. After a little while she started to graze.

'She's all right now,' Ciotóg said. 'You needn't be a bit anxious about her.'

'Thanks be to You, God,' I said, 'who sent ye in our path. Otherwise 'tis unknown how the story would end. We were petrified with dread at the thought of facing Séamas. Now we won't let on a word and in God's name let none of ye tell him but as little.'

'No fear!' Ciotóg said.

'Off home with ye now. And success to ye!' we told them.

Those three same men would lift even a heavier load than the beast that same day, for their equals weren't in the parish of Ballyferriter at that time.

They hopped into the cart and off they went taking the road to the north while Seáinín and myself faced for Dingle. When we arrived home there wasn't a syllable out of either of us. But what do you say to one of the women who was in the car if she didn't land in the following Saturday to tell Nell how concerned she had been and there wasn't one word I uttered that evening about the beast that she hadn't on the tip of her tongue! Women can go beyond all bounds; they are the very devil himself for causing disturbance. But what Nell said was that she was expecting a half-glass of whiskey and she wasn't one bit thankful to her for all her 'civility!'

I Return to My People

My health failed, I return home — The beauty of the countryside and the sea — How Tadhg Óg's house was burned down

I woke early one morning, stretched my limbs and looked around me. It was still early in the day and I had plenty of time to think. I considered that life was an odd place indeed and that one goes through many a twist and turn from the time of youthful folly until the hour of one's death.

'This is my last morning in this room,' I told myself. 'Someone else will sleep here tomorrow. But, God help me, I haven't an notion what the future holds for me.'

I looked across at Nan; she was sleeping soundly without, as they say, rent, stress or regret to bother her at that time.

'The latter end of *your* life is good!' I said in my own mind, 'no matter what way it was at the beginning. I suppose it was hard enough, just like my own case now, so maybe the end of my life will also prove good if God is willing!'

With that I heard the clock strike seven. 'No time now to be pondering on these things,' I told myself. 'But I'll be lonely leaving this house.'

By this time my mind was made up to pay a visit home — this because I wasn't feeling up to the mark. So I threw on my clothes and went down to the kitchen. Before long Séamas came downstairs after me.

'I hear you'll be going home today, Margaret,' he said.

'Yes! If my father comes to town.'

'Just as well for you!' Séamas said. 'Home is the best place to recover your health. It's hard for a person to work when he's not strong enough.'

By this time breakfast was ready and we were all sitting at the table. Everyone was eating and everyone was silent.

'We're all quiet, Margaret,' Nell said. 'We'll all be lonely after you because you've been in the house for a long while.'

'I'll be lonely too,' I said and I came very near to crying.

'I wouldn't be a bit bothered if I were going home in good form,' I said then, 'but the worst part of my story is that I'm not. And I don't know if ever again I will.'

'Don't say that!' Nell said. 'You'll be as right as rain before long.'

She left me and went out to the shop and I was clearing the table and putting away the delf. I got a start when I heard my father outside talking to Nell; although I was sad at first a kind of joy came over me when I saw him.

Nell spoke from outside. 'Get a cup of tea for your father. He's here!'

While my father was eating, Nell had a lot of 'bits and pieces' tied up in a bundle for me.

'You may as well get ready now, child,' she told me.

'However long the day is, night must fall,' I told myself, 'and my hour too has come.'

I went to where I kept my clothes; to be candid I hadn't very many of them so it was only too easy for me to string them together.

It was getting late in the day then and as there was a right long road before us it was just as well for us to be on our way. We had neither cart nor motor-car, so we had to depend on shank's mare.

Séamas and Nell were in the shop when I went out with my shawl across my shoulders. I got a pain in my heart with lonesomeness. I ran towards them and put my two hands around Nell's neck and no daughter ever kissed a mother as fondly as I kissed Nell that day. No wonder I did, because she was a mother to me when I was young and she remained a close friend of mine until the day of her death. God grant her soul eternal life!

I said goodbye to Séamas and, of course, to Seáinín and Eibhlín. They were crying bitterly. Then, as Oisín

111

said long ago, I turned my back on the land and faced straight as an arrow for the west.

My father and I were shortening our road and he was yarning away about a great many places so that we didn't find the journey long until we came to *Carraig an Phréa-cháin* and there I caught the first glimpse of Dunquin. The evening was lovely and we sat down on the verge of the road for a little while. I was looking all round me and I could see many things that held my interest. As far as I could see to the west the sea was like a sheet of glass. There wasn't a puff of wind in the sky but a tiny stir of breeze from the west brought me the wholesome smell of the sea. As for the sun it was a golden disc going in hide in the shadow of *Barra Liath*. Precisely at that moment a ray of light issuing from it moved directly eastward across the bay and the glimmering of that lance of light on the ocean resembled tiny particles of silver.

'It's true, what is said,' I told my father. 'There's no place finer than home!'

'True it is, child,' he said. 'Wherever a person is reared—that's the place he'd rather be.'

He was right, for despite the fact that Vicarstown was the most westerly townland in Ireland and also the most remote, that's where I'd prefer to be that night. If indeed the place lacked disturbance, noise and confusion it had peace, company and grace, for when the people would come together at night after their day's work you'd love to listen to them; some of them storytelling, others singing and others reminiscing about a way of life that had vanished. One who likes that type of company would certainly feel completely at home among them.

It was quite late in the evening when we went in home. My mother was delighted! She came to meet me, her two arms widespread and what a welcome she gave me! Cáit was milking the cows but when she came in she also gave me a very hearty welcome.

'*Sha!*' I said in my own mind. 'What one dreads, never happens, for I was certain that you'd give me a poor

112

welcome. But such isn't the case.' Cáit was cheerful and bright and it didn't take her long to prepare supper for us.

I had sweet cake that Nell had given me—something my mother always liked. I couldn't help laughing when I remembered the sweet cake I stole from Ould Kitty many years before but needless to say I didn't enlighten anyone as to why I was laughing!

Before the meal was finished the house had filled up with young people and grown-ups. That's a custom country-people have: to visit the house to welcome a stranger. To be sure, I was the stranger that night because everything I clapped eyes on somehow seemed strange to me. For example, I almost tumbled head over heels negotiating the bumps on the floor, and you must believe me when I say that the others were laughing and joking at me. But that made no matter; I was as contented as if I was in a palace. They had talk and company and fun for the rest of the night.

As for the old people they had their own kind of conversation by the fireside and I'd rather be listening to them than to the sweetest music ever played because I was keenly interested in their fine tales about the old heroes of legend.

A fair share of the morning had slipped by when I got up but I had no worry now. If I may say so, I had a taste of freedom and I had a mind to derive pleasure from that same freedom, but that wasn't an easy task for a person who didn't feel so well.

'I may as well get up,' I told myself, 'and ramble out in the air. Out-of-doors is where I'll best regain my health.'

I took with me a stocking that lay on the window and I sat on the fence and began to knit. It was a lovely time of day; the sun was shining and everything was peaceful. Above my head the birds were singing gaily. The sound of the river went harmoniously on and on as the water fell, making its own sweet music as it slid downwards over a bed of gravel and pebbles. Yonder stood the high peak that marked the shoulder of Mount Eagle; it looked splendid and attractive with something of elegance about it and the clean fragrant wind from the ocean combing its golden locks. I was listening to the river and watching the great giant mountain that stood right in front of me and my heart rose because I had seldom seen a sight as splendid during the four previous years.

Whatever look I gave, I saw a mighty vessel approaching from the north. The moment was one of rare peace; not a movement on the sea and because it was so calm I could see the reflection of the ship clearly. It was cleaving its way with dignity and the sea sped aft past its sides as the vessel parted the waters. 'Praised be God forever!' I told myself. 'The ocean is truly powerful when one considers that it can carry a load as mighty as that immense ship on its surface.' I kept watching the vessel until it passed through Blasket Sound and moved away to the south. I was conscious of nothing until my mother spoke from behind me. 'You have sunshine here, girl.' she said, as she sat down on the fence beside me.

She plied me with questions and I answered them as best I could. It was now close to dinner-time and great columns of smoke were rising from the houses.

'Isn't there a great deal of smoke rising from Keating's house?' I said. 'Maybe it's on fire!'

'God forbid!' my mother answered. Then: 'I well remember, girl, that there was smoke—and flame too—the time Tadhg Óg's house was burned down. God bless all those who hear the tale!'

'Bless us, indeed, how was it burned?' I asked. 'And did the people all die in the fire?'

'They died in the fire, darling,' she said. 'A family of seven who were in the house and a married couple who had no connection with the place at all were burned to death. Others too were badly burned but they didn't die.'

'Dear God! What did the mother do? Or did she survive?'

'She survived, child. But she was a mental wreck and no wonder she was. Father Manning was Parish Priest of Ballyferriter in those days; he was sent for and when he arrived on the scene he was appalled. No one could approach Cáit Mitchel—the mother of the family—but when the priest came he spoke softly to her in the hope that she would respond to him. She found it very difficult to heed him for she was tearing her hair and repeating over and over: "What have I left now but a poor bent old man?" The priest had pity and compassion for her and he went towards her saying: "Come and give me your hand." By the grace of God she came and stretched out her hand to the priest. "God's blessing on you, my poor woman, and the grace of patience," he said.

'"Father!" she said, "don't mention patience now! Not one was left alive!"

'"You have enough left yet with the help of God," the priest told her. "Promise me that you'll have patience and that you'll carry your cross and I give you my word that you'll be comfortable until the end of your days. Your daughter in America—I'll send for her: I'll tell her to come home to you and I'll do my best for you in every possible way I can. But promise me that you won't create a scene."

115

'"I promise you, Father, from my heart out, and from my mouth too that I'll do my very best."'

'He then told some of the women to take her with them and see after her.'

'Did the daughter come home?' I asked.

'She did, child,' my mother replied. 'That's her below in Ballyickeen married to Tomás Moriarty. Cáit Mitchel, her mother, she's the old woman with a good life now and her daughter's family are around her just as the priest had promised. As for the young married couple who were burned,' she went on, 'they met a dreadful end.'

'Wasn't it terrible to think,' I said, 'that the pair of them were burned to death. What happened them? Or what set the house on fire at all?'

'People were backward at that time, child, and they knew nothing at all about paraffin or any other kind of oil. Tadhg Óg and another man came across a barrel of paraffin washed up on some beach and they brought it to Tadhg Óg's house because his was the nearest to the cliff-top. It was a small house with only one door and the day they were dividing the oil a crowd of people arrived with jugs to get some of it. As it was being poured into the vessels some of it spilled on the litter on the floor and some time later a person lighted a rushlight to see if there was much oil left in the vessel. Alas, when he threw down the rush, the sudden blaze the litter and the barrel made as they exploded together came like a burst of thunder and lightning. Those who were able-bodied and were near the doorway got out by some means or other. A husband was outside while his wife was inside being burned alive; she was calling wildly for 'Séamas!' When he heard her he didn't care whether he lost his life or not, for she was the loveliest woman in Dunquin and the mother of his two children, so he tried to force his way through the flames to save her! Alas, neither he nor his wife ever again came out—nor many more like them. Often afterwards in the beginning of summer when the grandmother would have the two children she'd sing for them. This was her song:

My loved ones and my treasure,
My flawless pair in pleasure,
Now bloom in golden measure,
All summer flowers in prime,
But your bright flowers are withered . . .'

'God protect us! It was a terrible misfortune,' I said.
'Fate exists, child,' my mother answered.
Her storytelling ended as we were called in to the dinner.

Séamas who was called
'Pléasc'

How Pléasc defrauded his brother — Many years of roguery — How Pléasc made a match for a young lady of noble family — How he set a house on fire — The 'search' for the sheep

WHILE we were having a meal my father began to talk.

'Is it true that Muiris Scanlon and his family are leaving for America?' he asked.

'It is, I suppose,' Cáit said. 'Máire Sheáin was telling me today that the house and land will be up for auction.'

'Well, well! Isn't it a queer kind of a notion for him to be setting out for America in the latter end of his days?'

'What does he want here for?' Cáit asked. 'Aren't all his family over there? And when none of them would stay with him isn't it just as well for him to follow them?'

'I suppose you're right. When will the auction be?'

'The beginning of next month,' Cáit said.

I was listening to them and in my own mind I was thinking that it would be a happy day for me if I were going off with Muiris—but there was no possibility of that happening. When the meal was finished each one took on his own task and worked at it until it was dark; we were sitting round the fire when Jim rambled in with a class of a stoop on his back.

'Blessing of God here!' he said.

'The same to you,' Cáit replied.

'Seldom with ye be so lonely,' he commented.

'The company didn't arrive yet,' I said.

He wasn't long seated when he noticed a parcel on the window-sill.

'New boots! Seán brought them with him,' Cáit said.

He took the parcel and stripped off the paper.

'The dickens to it!' he said. 'I'd badly need a pair of these.'

'They're good boots,' said Cáit, '—except for the soles.'

'That's exactly what's wrong with them,' Jim said. 'The gutta-percha soles are no damn good.'

My father was filling his pipe with tobacco. I noticed that he was laughing.

'What's making you laugh?' I asked him.

'I'll tell you, then!' he said. 'Your man and the boots remind me of Séamas na bPléasc the night his brother brought home the boots from Dingle under his oxter. The brother was so scrupulous about them that he wouldn't put them on. But after he arrived home, Pléasc walked in the door.

'"You never put on the boots, Dónal?" he said.

'"I didn't," Dónal answered. "I was lighter for the road without them."

'"I'd take my oath that's not the real reason! You were terrified you'd wear them out," said Pléasc. Then: "I wonder would they fit me."

'"Likely they would," Dónal said; he was eating at the time.

'Pléasc threw off the tattered old brogues he was wearing and pulled on Dónal's boots. He stuck his hands into his britches' pockets and began whistling *An Samhradh Cruaidh*. Then off he goes with every jump out of his four bones on the flag of the hearth. And I promise you,' my father went on, 'that he knocked tally-ho out of the flag-stone with the boots. When Dónal had his food eaten he noticed that Pléasc was wearing his boots.

'"The devil fire your ribs," he shouted, "you stump of a fool. Would those be my boots you've on you?"

'"Dead right, my son!" Pléasc replied. "Have you never heard it said that what a person saves to wear his enemy lives to tear.'

'Dónal was in a flaming temper. Séamas took off the boots and went off out the door whistling softly; he left Dónal still cursing away and massaging the boots with the palm of his hand.'

'Nothing was a match for Pléasc,' Jim commented.

'You never spoke a truer word!' said my father. 'He was a proper playboy. He'd pretend to be a fool, but the people knew that Pléasc was what is called an "iron fool." One day he went off to Dingle with a firkin of butter and I suspect that the butter wasn't too good because the poor man had only the one cow. Two other men from the same district went with him and they had butter too. The firkins were ranged out in the buttermarket and the men weren't long waiting until the buyer came along. He first plunged the butter-borer into Séamas's firkin. Pléasc caught a firm grip of his wrist and said:

> *Butter-Taster, darling dear*
> *Don't drive your butter-borer low*
> *For even the seagull on the pier*
> *Knows that the dregs are down below.*
> *With nanny-goat's milk I've brimmed my barrel*
> *For Landlord Rice holds my cows in pawn*
> *So if this butter reneges my cattle*
> *They'll never again see freedom's dawn.*

'"I don't care if the devil himself is down there!" the buyer said, and he gave top price for the firkin. Pléasc was more than satisfied and he had a great laugh at the expense of the others.'

'I never heard a proper account of him until this night.' Jim said. 'Was he married?'

'Sure, he was married!' my father replied, 'and he had a fine wife—Peig Bhán was her name. I'd say that he was jealous of her, and that that was his reason for leaving home and going away to Ballygoleen. He left her there, herself and her family of three, and spent fourteen years in Ballygoleen working for the old Lord. And I'd say that in all that time Pléasc was doing more to the detriment of Lord Ventry than he was to promoting his welfare. He wasn't too keen on lords at all because it was people of that class who had given himself and his relations "the

120

high road and the wattle". So it didn't cost Pléasc a thought to steal some of their property whenever he'd get the chance for the old man was a simple-minded gentleman who took Pléasc's word for everything.

'He wasn't very long in Ballygoleen,' my father went on, 'when a young lady came visiting to the Great House. A few days afterwards a young man of good family arrived—his name was McWalter. He was trying to get the young lady to marry him but she never fancied him at all and indeed it never entered her head that he'd follow her to Ballygoleen. It didn't take Pléasc long to discover why she was there and he took it on himself to interest himself in her affairs. Hardly a day passed that he didn't get a chance of chatting with her so that he wormed out every detail of her private affairs.

'At that time there was a handsome manly boy of the Fitzgeralds in Dingle and Séamas knew him well. One day they happened to meet and Pléasc began telling him the whole story about the lady. The young man listened carefully until Pléasc had finished.

The upshot of the matter was that Pléasc never stopped until he had introduced the pair to each other; they fell in love at once and it was always Pléasc who arranged their appointments.

'By this time the lady had spent three months in the Great House and McWalter was all the while watching her like a cat watching a mouse but unknown to the unfortunate man there was a conspiracy afoot right under his nose. Fitzgerald was making all the arrangements and Pléasc was giving him a helping hand. When matters were fully arranged Pléasc spoke to the lady.

'"Be ready tonight," he told her. "A person will arrive for you some time during the morning hours. And if you can steal away without raising a fuss you'll be lucky."

'"That suits me!" she said.

'Pléasc didn't lie on any bed that night but kept a watch-out for the lady. About two o'clock in the morning Fitzgerald came with a suitable coach. Pléasc went to the window of the room where the young woman slept; she had everything ready and had nothing to do but throw her belongings into the coach. She slipped out quietly; Fitzgerald took her in his arms, settled her into the vehicle and away they flew!

'Pléasc went to sleep for himself and a fair share of the morning had gone by before he got up. Everyone he met had the same story; the lady had stolen away from the House! Pléasc pretended that he didn't know a thing about it—no more than anyone else.

'MacWalter then left the Great House in the deepest possible despair and his head was in a proper whirl. He had no idea how the lady had succeeded in getting away unknown to him, considering the close watch he kept on her.'

'I'd say,' said Jim, 'that Pléasc came well out of it after the fine way he worked for them.'

'You can bet your life he did,' said my father.

'I'd say too,' said Jim, 'that Pléasc held his job in Ballygoleen all the while.'

'He did that too!' said my father. 'And he wasn't idle there. Often he'd persuade the old Lord that black was white. The old man had the makings of a race-horse at that time—a young colt and very proud the old boyo was of him! He called the horse "Bang Up." When Pléasc realized that the old fellow was so attached to the animal some devil or other picked him and he made up his mind to do the colt harm—if only he could get the chance of doing so. One night he cornered the colt in Reenbeg headland and he never cried halt until he drove the animal down over the cliff and put him swimming in the sea. Then he hurried off to the Great House.

'The old Lord had a habit of walking out early in the morning before his breakfast and he saw Pléasc approaching. Pléasc had his jacket off and there was a mad stare in his eye.

'"What's wrong with you, Séamas?" the old Lord asked in Irish, for he could speak the language well.

'"God relieve us!" said Pléasc. "'Bang Up' is drowned."

'"Tck-tck-tck! That's bad news," said the old Lord. "What's to be done now?"

'"I came to get a sheaf of oats," Pléasc said. "Maybe when he sees the oats he'll head for the land."

'To lay eyes on him at that time,' my father went on, 'you'd take your oath that there wasn't a crooked bone in his body. The rogue pretended that he himself was more concerned than anyone about the affair and that he was a fool into the bargain.'

'There is no limit to the crookedness of some people,' said Jim. 'Pléasc was well able to put his roguery across on the gentleman. There's a lot of his kind in the country-side.'

'My word, but he was a polished trickster,' said my father. 'Did you hear how he burned down the gardener's house?'

'I never heard a word about it,' said Jim.

'The gardener was a middle-aged man,' said my father, 'and he had a neat comfortable house in the garden. Pléasc slept with him in this house and one day he had reason to suspect that the gardener had a couple of pounds in silver in the pocket of his britches and he didn't know from Adam how to come around the money. If he stole it he'd be certain to be caught because there was nobody else to take it. Do you know the plan he thought of? To set fire to the house and then maybe he'd get his hands on the money by some means or other.

'One night the pair were in bed for some time but Pléasc hadn't the faintest intention of going to sleep because the rascal was bent on roguery. The poor gardener was snoring away. Pléasc put his hand gently under the gardener's head for that was where the other fellow kept his trousers. Pléasc drew it towards him, caught it by the ends and began to shake it.

'"What's up with you?" the gardener asked.

'"Those mice have me out of my mind," said Pléasc. "The house is alive with them; with that he gave the trousers a mighty shake—to frighten the mice, by the way! Just then the gardener heard his silver jingling as it dropped out of his trousers' pocket.

'"*Aililiú*, my money!" he said. He got a right fright because he wouldn't trust Pléasc as far as he'd throw him.

123

'"Get up out of that," the gardener said, "and light a sop of straw."

'All Pléasc wanted was an excuse. He hopped out of bed and pulled on his trousers. The poor gardener was peering out at him with a worried expression on his face. Pléasc lighted a wisp of straw but before long it quenched. He lighted wisp after wisp but that sort of light was no use to the gardener who, by this time, was down on all fours groping in the litter. He snapped at Pléasc and told him to light a bigger piece of straw. So Pléasc gathered a big bundle of straw and set fire to it.

'"That's it, man! Hold it high!" said the gardener.

'Indeed it didn't take Pléasc long to lift up the bundle fine and high in such a way that the roof of the house caught fire. Then there was a right racket and hubbub—the cabin in flames, the money gone, and those inside maybe burned and scorched.

'"The devil sweep your soul, you fool, you have the house on fire!" the gardener shouted.

'"Serve it right if it's scorched and scalded," said Pléasc, "aren't you the fault of it yourself? You weren't satisfied with a small blaze and now you aren't satisfied with a big blaze!" And off he marched out the door.

'"For God's sake, help me with my feather-bed!" the gardener screeched after him.

'"I own to God!" said Pléasc, "your life is more important to you than that!"

'"Give me a hand with the bed!" the gardener pleaded.

'Pléasc came back and caught the head of the tick while the gardener took hold of the other end. The tick got jammed between the two doorposts with Pléasc outside and the gardener inside. According as the gardener would push it out, Pléasc would push it in, for he hadn't the slightest scrap of sympathy for the unfortunate gardener. All he wanted was, by fair means or foul, to lay hands on the money. So he kept the gardener inside until every rib of his beard was singed.

'When day dawned for the poor gardener he left Ballygoleen and he has never been seen there since. When the fire was quenched Pléasc had everything as he wanted it and he began at the smouldering edge of the blaze and kept on rooting until he had recovered every penny of the gardener's money. Needless to say he was delighted.'

'That he may be hanged and throttled,' Jim said. 'He was a patent robber.'

'He was full of roguery at any rate,' said my father. 'He spent six days of the week setting potatoes at home in Kilvickadownig—and drew his week's hire as well.'

'He must have found it hard to have his cake and eat it,' Jim said.

'Not at all, man,' said my father, 'for he was able to persuade the old Lord into believing anything. He stole six sheep from him and in the dead of the night he hoisted them off to Kilvickadownig and tied them inside in a garden he had there. That done he came back to his own door and rapped on it.'

'"Who's there?" his wife asked.

'"Me!" said Séamas. "Open up."

'She got up and let him in. "Almighty Father! What brought you this hour of the night?" she asked.

'"It's all the damn same to you," Pléasc said. "But tell the lads to be sure to mind the sheep in the garden and not to give anyone a tittle of information as to how they got there."

'"Don't worry," said Peig, his wife.

'"I'll likely be back again about ten o'clock," said Pléasc, "I have no business delaying now."

'He clapped a red coal of fire on his pipe, took to his two heels and indeed fear or fright of the night didn't bother him. He was a great deal more in dread that he'd meet a live person who'd cross-hackle him. But he met no one; when he reached Ballygoleen he stole up to bed very quietly without anyone hearing him.

'The following morning when the shepherd got up, he was told that six of the sheep were missing. He hadn't the faintest idea how they had left the rest of the flock but, of course, robbers were numerous at that time and they could have stolen the sheep. But how on earth could the shepherd face the steward and tell him that the sheep were gone? He knew well that the steward would be raging

125

with him but whatever way the wind blew he'd have to tell him!

'When he told his tale to the steward the latter said that a thorough search should be mounted for the sheep before coming to the conclusion that a thief had stolen them. While the shepherd and the steward were chatting, Pléasc came along and enquired what they were discussing.

'"Six fat sheep gone from the shepherd last night," the steward said, "and he doesn't know whether they're stolen or gone astray."

'Pléasc was thinking over this for a while; then he said to the steward, "If I thought I'd draw my day's pay while I was doing so, I'd scour every nook, hole, and field from here to Com Aille in search of them. And I wouldn't be weary nor lazy either!"

'"Don't be a bit worried on that score, Séamas," said the steward. "You'll draw your pay for I'd prefer to get back the sheep than accuse poor people of robbery."

'"Fair enough, my respectable man,' said Pléasc. And off he went and never drew bit nor bridle until he arrived at Kilvickadownig. He took hold of his spade, carried it up to the garden and spent the day working almost until dusk. By the time he had a bite of food eaten it was dark. He went out, tied a light rope to one of the sheep and drove her before him until he brought her to the shepherd. The shepherd was pleased and thanked Pléasc.

'"Maybe," Pléasc said, "I could find the rest of them too."

'He spent the week working for his family, and every night he'd bring a sheep with him back to Ballygoleen.'

'Isn't it amazing that no one found him out?' Jim said.

'They didn't in the beginning,' said my father. 'But in the end the steward got kind of suspicious and began asking people questions about Pléasc. The upshot of the affair was that he found out every single detail about poor Pléasc and he hunted him home. That finished him with Ballygoleen! The poor man was at home then,' went on my father, 'with little to do! And when anyone would question him about it he'd say, "Ah, my son, even a noble horse can't run well for ever!"'

A Feast, an Escort and a Farewell Forever

A neighbouring family leaves for America — An 'American wake' — The convoy — 'It won't be long until I send you the fare'

WHAT'S seldom seen is much admired: this statement could be applied to the people of Dunquin. Not very many of them had ever seen an auction and now the only topic of conversation was the auction day, for Muiris's land was to be put up for sale on Tuesday and we'd have a great day's entertainment.

On Tuesday morning the auctioneer arrived and every man and boy in the parish had gathered at the place where the auction was to be held. A large number of people were interested in buying the land but because it was in a very remote townland no one from outside the parish was bidding. Pádraig Scanlon, Muiris's brother, bought the place, for he happened to have the cash—a thing very few people had at that time.

Muiris was thoroughly satisfied with the day's work. Ever and always he was bent on going to America but he didn't realize his dream until now. By the time it was dark, Muiris had sent out invitations to all the old neighbours to come and have a social night together. He had a barrel of porter and a gallon of whiskey and you can take it from me that with songs and good company we had what amounted to a minor wedding. For part of the night too, the young people held a dance.

Nothing would satisfy Muiris except to invite my mother. They were next-door neighbours and there never had been a cross word between them so that my mother was very very sorry to see him go.

127

'Off with you!' he told me, 'and call in your mother. We'll have tonight's company together whatever comes or goes.'

Off I went, and of course, the poor woman was delighted. She was a person who revelled in company—may she and all the holy souls be at peace.

When she arrived, Muiris welcomed her and put her sitting on a chair beside the fire. He brought along a jug of whiskey and filled out a glass for her.

'Here!' he said. 'Drink my health! We'll never drink another glass together on this side of the grave!'

My mother took the glass in her hand.

'Here's a health to you all!' she cried, 'and especially a health to Muiris, my gentle honest neighbour of old who never caused a neighbour's child to cry not to mind coming to my door in anger.'

When Muiris made the rounds a second time with the jug he didn't forget the old lady. But I swear to you that she soon got her speech and before very long she had started to sing *Na Bearta Cruadha* and she was bringing vibrations from the ridging of the house! Many a person said that in her day there wasn't a finer singer in Kerry than my mother.

'My soul, Muiris,' said I, 'the poet was right when he said:

> *The old crone crippled with gout*
> *Thrown in the corner in pain,*
> *If she drained but a fourpenny glass*
> *Her joints would dance once again.*

'Will you look at my mother now,' I went on, 'you couldn't imagine that there was a thing in the world wrong with her.'

'That's the way life goes, my girl,' Muiris said. 'She had a great heart if it wasn't for her lack of health.'

Then the dancing started at the other end of the house and we had revelry and applause till day brightened in the east. Time then for everyone to be making for his own home. I took my mother by the hand and led her away with me. A good part of the day had slipped by when she woke the following day.

At last the day dawned when Muiris and his family were bidding their last good-bye to the neighbours. We had a custom at that time for everyone in the parish, great and small, to 'convey' the person who was going to America. The excitement and noise wakened me in the morning. Such running and racing! A large number of his relations were calling at Muiris's house that morning to bid him farewell.

I got up quickly because I had a number of small jobs to see after. I had my mind now made up that from the moment my health improved I'd go into service again— that is if I got a suitable place. There was nothing to be gained by remaining at home, for however long I stayed there, all I'd get in the end was the road. So I realized that it would be better for me to turn a penny for myself and not to depend on anyone else. And another thing that forced me to a decision was this: Cáit-Jim was going to America with Muiris and she had promised me that she'd send me the passage-money as soon as she possibly could, and it would be advantageous for myself too if I had something put aside towards the fare when my own day would arrive.

I told no one what was on my mind but I was ready to accompany Muiris to Dingle. All the morning there was great activity; some people were crying and others were laughing. It's a sad occasion when a person leaves for America; it's like death for only one out of a thousand ever again returns to Ireland. Is it any wonder then that the emigrants' relations are troubled and upset when their own folks are leaving?

We had neither horse nor side-car; all we had was Jim's horse and common car and that was full of luggage. But whether or no, there was room for Muiris—the rest of us walked.

By the time we moved up the Well Road one would think that it was a funeral procession. The Dunquin people had the custom in those days of 'conveying' whoever was going to America as far as the stone heap known as the Leacht. We moved along the road, some of us downhearted and others in good spirits until we reached the top of the Clasach. Then or never there was a right scene; the parting of friends was a sorrowful sight, for parted they were from that day forward as surely as if they were buried in a grave, for none of them ever again met the other. Those who were not going to Dingle said good-bye to those who were leaving and then they turned their backs on one another; one band of people faced for home and the other for the Dingle Road.

We had a long walk before us but it made no matter since there was a crowd of us together and we never felt the journey until we reached Dingle. We made straight for Galvin's for he was the Booking Agent for America at that time. Those who were travelling had to see after a lot of things—travelling cases and various odds and ends for the following day. I remained with them all the while and when night fell a great crowd of people had gathered into the house for those who were going away were to stay there until morning. There was plenty of company in the house that night for Mr. Galvin was a sociable man on his own floor and we had music and dancing and song until midnight so that we never felt the time passing until at last the man of the house said that it was time to go to bed as we'd have to be up early in the morning. Then the music came to an end and everyone began to think about sleep.

At seven o'clock the following morning the little bell on the alarm clock rang and everyone did his best to get dressed so as to be ready for the breakfast. But not many of them felt like eating or drinking as they were too over-come with sorrow.

About ten o'clock they were ready to leave and we said good-bye to one another. I was very lonely after Cáit-Jim. Why wouldn't I be, for she was my loyal comrade ever since I was a child! Needless to say, I was crying but this is what she said to me:

'Don't fret one bit, girl, for if God leaves me my health it won't be long until I send you the fare. Good-bye now,' she said, and then she herself began to cry.

Before I had time to wipe the tears from my eyes they were all swept out of my sight. That was the last time we laid eyes on one another.

In Service again

A visit to my old employer — I find a new one — A hard life and a hard-hearted woman — The cow I neglected to tie — Myself and the servant boy

EVERYONE has his own concern and I was no exception to the rule. As I have already mentioned, I was determined, if I got another place in service, not to return home. With this in mind I walked up the street in Dingle and went in to see Nell; as soon as she saw me she welcomed me. There was no one in the house but herself and another woman with whom she was in conversation. Nell had her bosom down on the counter and the pair were chatting away as I entered.

'You've some business in Dingle today, Máiréad?' Nell asked.

'You may say that!' I answered. 'Did you ever hear the expression "A master looking for a servant boy and a servant boy looking for a master"?'

'I often did,' Nell said.

'I came to see if you had any account of where I'd get a place in service.' Nell gave a short laugh.

'That's a coincidence!' she said. 'Maybe yourself and Bríghdín here would strike a bargain'—she was referring to the woman standing at the counter. This woman turned to me and said: 'You might as well come along with me. I badly need a girl like you and I'll give you eight pounds from this till the end of twelve months.'

I kind of knew her already and I had the impression that she was a very nice-mannered woman; but as an old saying goes: 'The proof of the pudding is in the eating!' At any rate we made the bargain and there was no more to be said until I was standing waiting in the doorway. She and her husband had a horse and cart in Dingle; they took me with them and it didn't take us long to reach the house.

The minute I entered the house it was as if the darkness of the world came down over me for I knew that once again I was in slavery. But if that was the case, I had to control my feelings. My mistress quickly prepared a meal and we sat down to the table together. She cross-examined me about housework and I told her that I could do anything in the world except milk cows—this because I never had the occasion to milk one.

'That won't matter,' she told me. 'You'll be well able to milk by the end of a month.'

I threw off my shawl and I can tell you that I was strong and capable doing my jobs around that house from that day forward. It didn't take me long to learn how to milk the cows and to do a number of other tasks too; I had more than enough to cope with since there was no servant boy about the place. The result was that I had to work both inside and outside.

I wasn't there long until I realized that Bríghdín wasn't all she was reported to be for I often had the rumblings of hunger in my guts with no possible chance of getting a bite of food until it was well past time for a meal. Often too I'd tell myself that her main stock in trade was soft talk with very little to back it. That woman hadn't the heart of a mouse! What a difference between her and Nell, for Nell was one great-souled woman!

But there was no use brooding over that now. Hope was keeping me up; if I could only battle on until the end of the year—until such time as Cáit-Jim could send me my passage-money and I also had enough earned on my own, things would be easier for me. So I reined in my feelings and kept plodding away.

My boss was as good as gold but like many another man before him he wasn't boss on his own floor. I had a great deal to do with the cows and he always held one special threat over my head—to tie them properly because it was highly dangerous if one of them managed to free herself. There was a long beam of timber running from gable to gable in the cow-house with one chain and staple through it for each of the cows. There were ten cows in the stall and there were two doors to the building. The doors were seldom closed unless the weather was really bad.

One Saturday the man of the house was in Dingle and I had to look after the cows that evening. I daresay, simply because I had a great deal on hands, I didn't do my business properly. As the old proverb has it: "Master your trade or your trade will master you!" and how true that saying is! It was dark when the boss arrived home, his hat as usual skew-ways on the side of his head and neither cow nor calf bothering him extra much. When he had a bite of food eaten he rambled off to bed for himself.

I got up early the following morning and put my head to the door. Great God! what should I see but one of the cows out in the farmyard calmly chewing the cud. I couldn't describe to you the way my heart jumped with fright. I almost dropped life and I was trembling from head to foot. I was in pure terror of the man of the house and why wouldn't I?—for the one order he was forever dinging into my head was not to neglect a single cow when I'd be tying them. By now, I was absolutely certain that the cow had done damage and what excuse could I give him? I was at fault and my neglect had earned me blame. I'd be ashamed to return home with that sort of an apish story—not to mention all the harm my carelessness had caused.

But there was no use gabbling when the damage was done. I went up to the cow-house on legs that were hardly able to bear me up. When I stuck my head in to see what damage the cows had done they were lying down eating and chewing the cud—all except the cow nearest to the door; she was bleeding and hunched up as if she were about to die. 'You're finished, anyway, girl,' I told myself.

Then or never I was at my wits' end and I didn't know what best to do. I recalled something Nan had once told me: 'The greatest trouble you're in, Máiréad,' she said, 'call on God to help you and there will be no fear of you!'

'Almighty God!' I prayed, 'help me to think of some plan that'll save me from this calamity!'

Then the idea struck me that if I could pull out the staple from the beam of timber I could then tie the rope around the cow's head and no one would ever be the wiser but that she had pulled it free.

I got a class of plucky then and I caught hold of the rope; but, God of Graces! staple and beam were fixed as firmly as handle and mallet hewn from a single block. Tadhg Dhiarmada—the strongest man in the parish—wouldn't have pulled it the best day he ever was.

But it's true also that God is even stronger than all expectations. I tied the rope around my body and dug my two sturdy legs firmly into a foothold in the ground. But misfortune again, the staple wouldn't budge! I kept on swaying backwards and forwards and before long I felt it giving way. I was now in full fettle so I put all my strength into the job on hands, and the dickens take me, it was a wonder my brains weren't dashed out against the wall when the staple gave! I give you my word that I wouldn't have preferred a present of the whole parish at that particular moment. 'Thanks again and again to God,' I said, 'who relieves every hardship.'

Out I went to where the cow was; I tied the rope around her head and I'd defy anyone to discover what had happened. That done, I closed the door for fear she'd go back in again and do more harm. Down I went to the house with greater courage than before; I went to the room door and called the man of the house.

'What's wrong with you?' he said peevishly because he was still suffering from the effects of the drink.

'One of the cows is loose,' I said.

'Good God! I suppose she has damage done?'

'I think the roan cow is hurt anyhow,' I said.

Down he comes in a hurry and he was stepping so lightly that he wouldn't have broken eggs if they were under his feet. He didn't wait for shoe nor stocking for the poor man was in a right panic. I wouldn't blame him at all, as he had enough to do to make ends meet besides meeting misfortune like that. Off we went up to the cow-house, himself leading the way with a slight stoop on him, and there he went over to the injured cow and examined her. She was gored in the hindquarter but he made nothing of it. He went out to the cow in the farmyard and examined the tying on her head. There she was chewing the cud and the chain and staple were dangling loose from about her neck.

'I don't know from Adam how she pulled it free,' he said. 'I'd have sworn that it was so firm that the Great Eastern Cableship wouldn't have pulled it loose!'

He wouldn't have said that if he only knew all the puffing and blowing I had trying to pull it. But then again, I admit that it wasn't I pulled it, but the power of God when He saw me in the trouble.

My master was a hot-tempered contrairy man and there was no knowing what he'd do to me, but he had nothing to say on that occasion. I had come round on the blind side of him and he could attach no blame to me. But believe you me, I was never in a tight corner like that again as long as I remained under that roof for I paid the very best attention to everything I had to do.

One Saturday morning in early spring the boss of the house was in a state of great excitement. I knew well that he was going to Dingle for he was the type of man you could coax there on the slightest possible excuse. About ten o'clock he tackled the horse.

'Where are you going today?' I asked him.

'To see if I'd find any class of a servant boy,' he replied. 'There's a great deal of work to be done at this time of year and I might chance even to get a man to follow the horse, but then again it's hard to get that same because they're in great demand. And another thing, I'd like to take some of the load off your back.'

'God direct you to do the right thing always!' I said, rambling up the narrow little passageway that ran between the house and the backgarden.

By this time the woman of the house was ready to go with him for she didn't fancy his going off by himself when he had the horse, for as often as not he'd be half-drunk returning from Dingle, with the result that she'd be greatly worried about him. When they were ready to leave he drew a lash of the whip across the horse's back and off they went. There was nothing I preferred than to see them go because I had very little peace of mind while Bríghdín was around. She wasn't easy to please for she was tight-fisted—cranky too, and often so with some cause where I was concerned.

But whatever about that, it was evening-time before they returned and they had a big belter of a servant boy with them. When the man of the house came in: 'What do you think but I got him,' he said with a kind of bravado.

'Upon my soul, you have him!' I said, 'and a well-set strong scourger of a lad he is!'

'Right you are! And you won't have so much work to do now, with God's help.'

Fair enough! When the supper was ready we sat down. We were eating and drinking together contentedly for there was a kind of veneration for the servant boy. It is an old proverb: 'What's new in a house gets the most affection.'

From that out, I hadn't half the work to do although I'd often have to help out with certain jobs, for farmers have a great deal of work on hands in the springtime. We were passing away the time—sometimes things ran smoothly and other times it was the reverse until we had spent two months together. The servant boy was the devil and all of a whinger and often he and I weren't on the best of terms. But he was in dread of the man of the house.

One Sunday morning after I had returned from First Mass I had a woeful toothache and I was feeling as disgruntled as a pig. The man and woman of the house had gone off to Second Mass. I wanted to light a fire and I told the boy who was standing at the doorway filling his pipe to bring me a little basket of turf from the rick. He looked at me sourly and said: 'That's woman's work!'

'I wouldn't have asked you only I have a toothache that's driving me out of my mind,' I said.

'To blazes with you and your rotten teeth!'

'Erra, man dear, a full tide of anger took me, for his bitter answer had wounded me to the quick. I caught up a half-rotten turnip that lay beside me and I flung it at him, and where did I strike him but right into the earhole! The turnip was plastered to the side of his skull and that I may be dead, if he were to stab me with a knife I couldn't help laughing at him, although he was not to be trifled with at that particular time for he ran towards me with his fist closed ready to strike me.

'Watch out, boy! Don't strike me or you'll be the worse for it!' I shouted.

'The devil blister your hide for you,' he said, turning on his heel.

I took up the little basket and as I was returning with the turf he came out the door against me with a parcel under his arm.

'There you are, my bucko!' I told him, 'if I had rotten teeth a while ago the side of your head is rotten now'—I said this because the mark of the turnip was still on the side of his face.

He didn't say one word but put a scowl on him. His head was as red as a turkey-cock with the dint of bad temper.

When the man of the house came home he called the servant boy to untackle the horse, but alas! the servant boy wasn't to be found, nor trace nor tidings of him but as little. We didn't know where he had gone to: all we knew was that he had taken his old rags with him. Even though the woman of the house suspected that there had been some quarrel between him and me I assure you that I didn't give her any information on the subject but let her find it out from some other source.

My Last Days in
Service

*The laughter of the woman of the house — Searching for
the cattle — Bad news from home — A sad night's journey
home*

ONE mild, misty afternoon in the beginning of May the
woman of the house said to me after dinner:

'Drive down the calves, Máiréad, and we'll have them
seen to before you go after the cows.'

I went off and drove down eight young calves; when
they had finished drinking the milk she drove them out
to me.

'Drive them up again now,' she said, 'and make no
delay above!'

Because of the rainwater and the puddle, I had the
hem of my petticoat well taken up so as to avoid having it
like a dirty tail. As I was passing outside the kitchen
window I glanced in; my mistress was standing at the
table in roars of laughter. I took it that she was laughing
at me on account of my fleshy legs and the tied-up hem of
my petticoat so I put a surly face on myself. As I entered
the house she was in the same fit of laughing—it was as
if she had a bite of food in her mouth.

'Will I go for the cows?' I asked her.

She never pretended to hear me but kept her mouth
wide open in laughter.

'Blast it for a story!' I said. 'It's a queer turn in the
world indeed when you're ridiculing me who is as well-
bred as yourself. But it has always been said, "The
weakling as he can and the strong man as he covets!"'

I took the piece of stick in my hand and, disgruntled
enough, went off for the cows. When I came back with
them I heard din and uproar inside. I went in and what

did I see but the woman of the house whom I had left half an hour previously standing at the table breaking her heart laughing, as I thought, stretched out on the bed completely disabled and unable to utter a word.

'What in God's name knocked her out since then?' I asked myself.

No one knew what had come over her. She wasn't able to swallow a drink because her throat was tightly closed and we couldn't understand one word she uttered except what issued from gaps in the front of her mouth where a tooth had fallen out. Approaching daybreak, the man of the house had to go for the priest and doctor. The doctor was there first; a nurse came with him.

The evening was fairly advanced when the priest arrived: after he had prepared the woman for death the nurse showed him the woman's throat. He examined it carefully.

'Get me a linseed meal poultice,' he said.

This was done; the priest took it in one hand and made the sign of the cross on it with the other. Then he applied the poultice to the woman's throat. It wasn't there much more than a quarter of an hour when he told the nurse to remove it. When she had taken it off, there was—God between us and all harm!—what appeared to be a small snail like a periwinkle on the poultice.

'What will I do with it now, Father?' the nurse asked.

'Turn right around and clap that fire down on top of it."

Her ladyship improved from that moment: I'd often tell her when she annoyed me afterwards that the fairies had clodded her!

The summer was fine, sultry, and dry. Five or six cattle were grazing on the hillside field and as the weather was so fine they often had to be driven to water. After dinner-time the boss came in.

'Margaret,' he said, 'you may as well drive the cattle to water for they haven't had a drink for two days.' Although I was lazy enough to move off I had no business going against him. That was the reason I was there and earning my tuppenny pay! I stood up and called the puppy in the house; he was very useful, for I had him trained to catch the cattle by the tail and as soon as he'd pinch them they'd go wild. My master was often angry with me because the cows' tails were torn by the pup but that didn't bother me as long as it was convenient for myself.

Myself and my little dog moved upwards against the hill but when I reached the field, I couldn't find trace nor tidings of the beasts. I was in a hill field with a fairly sharp rise in it and when I went to the higher part of the field I still couldn't see them. They had wandered away out of the heat of the day. I didn't know what best to do but when I got to a point where I could see the other flank of the flat-topped hill, I spied a middle-aged man a little distance away from me. I went towards him and enquired if he had seen any strange cattle.

'A short while ago,' he said, 'they passed me over there. I think that they're in that ruin beyond.'

I went away feeling satisfied with myself, because I realized I could have been searching for them all day. I drove the cattle along until I came to a place where an old man was standing and he gave me a hand to drive them into the field. Only for that, it would have been a case of what happened in the old story—'A Journey to the Well at the World's End.' He was a very obliging man and I thanked him.

By the time I had reached the other side of the field I was as tired as a dog and sweat was pouring down off me, and indeed my little pup had a full bandle of his tongue hanging out of his mouth. The cattle were grazing away for themselves and I was in no great hurry.

I sat down on a level place where white bog-grass and heather were growing. It was a delightful spell of good weather and a pleasant cool puff of breeze was blowing; I gave the breeze full, free permission to caress me for I always loved the wind that blows from the sea and at that moment I welcomed it. It reminded me of the lovely gay days when Cáit-Jim and myself were going off with food to the men cutting turf on the hill. But we were a great distance apart on this day! Many a hill and glen, aye, and immense wave of the sea lay between us! She was in a foreign land, a lady if you please, with a ring on her finger and a watch in her pocket! I wondered if she was content, or was she remembering me as I was remembering her? Maybe she was even jealous of me! The flat-topped hill on which I sat was as pleasant as any part of Yankee-land and, as they say, 'Far-off hills are green but not always are they grassy.' If it were God's will and my destiny to find some little home in Ireland I'd never leave it as long as I lived.

A man, they say again, lives long in his native place. Is there a man in the world who wouldn't be moved by the sight that met my eyes—hundreds of hills thrusting their heads upwards behind each other; not far away lay fine level plains and green fragrant fields, men and women crouched working in those same fields, white seagulls clamorous in flight in the sky above their heads and now and again coming down to the earth to forage for food. Before my eyes lay the beautiful view that stretched from the saddle-pass of Ballynana to Brandon Creek and thence north to Kilquane Lake where the holy saint covered the monster with the cauldron. Thence again, all round to Ballygoleen where Pléasc spent fourteen years of his life in trickery and knavery and thence again to the point of Rinnbeg where Muiris O'Shea swam across as he escaped from the police; close to Rinnbeg lies Pouladav where, once upon a time, shipping galore entered the harbour. I had an excellent view across the bay as far as Iveragh; the sea was majestic and the sunlight was painting the water gold.

If I were a person who had the gift of truly describing the beauty of the scenery and of the pleasant nature of the land that lay about me I would indeed have a great deal to write down. I was like one under a spell and I didn't find the time slipping by. Then I sprang to my feet and stretched myself. I set the dog after the cattle but he paid me little heed; he moved off close to where they were and then sat down on his haunches! The more I gave him orders the lazier he became. You'd think he was mocking me. If I could only lay hands on him at that time I'd tear him asunder! I wore neither shoe nor stocking and since little else grew in the field except fine furze and heather, each tiny thorn was like a tailor's needle standing point-up after the heat of the day. Walking barefooted through the field was a real penance but I had nothing better to do than to risk it. Off I went through the field in the direction of the cattle and when they heard me coming towards them they set off at a run before me until they came to the gate. The pup knew that he had done wrong because no matter what soft talk I gave him he wouldn't come next nor near me.

By the time the cattle had reached the river I was far more in need of water than they were; I needed to plunge my feet into it for they were scalded from the furze. The man of the house was there before me and he told me to go home—that he'd drive up the cattle himself. When I reached the house my mistress had a dreadful scowl on her face.

'It's a pity you didn't stay longer,' she said.

In a way she was right but, at the same time, 'right' is often too harsh a judgement.

He who starts out with hardship for a comrade remains in its company; hardship was my comrade early enough in life and it still kept a firm grip on me. On Friday morning after breakfast the woman of the house called me. 'What do you want now?' I asked her when I came in.

'The boss is going to Dingle,' she answered. 'You might as well go with him and take a churn of milk.'

Naturally, I was delighted for I hadn't such an opportunity for a long time.

'What's the matter with yourself?' I enquired.

'I don't feel too well today; I have a headache,' she said.

'It's an ill wind that blows nobody good,' I said in my own mind.

The man of the house had the horse tackled in the farmyard and the churn was brought out. When it was filled with milk and everything was ship-shape we sat into the cart and it didn't take us long to reach Dingle; we travelled the lower road to the Mall: that was where the milk market was held. My boss untackled the horse and tied it to the side of a gate and gave it some hay. Then he moved off to do his own jobs and left me with the task of selling the milk. A woman stood in front of me with measures to dole out the milk to the buyers.

I had the last of my milk almost sold when I saw a man coming towards me from the west. His head was bent and he had an air of sorrow about him. He was a Dunquin man; he walked past me and before long I saw another man with the same sorrowful appearance. This second man was my brother Seán and I knew by the 'cut' of him that something was troubling him. I ran towards him and caught him by the hand.

'Is there something wrong at home, Seán?' I asked him.

'God help us,' he said, 'we have our share of trouble. Big Cáit died last night.'

Man! but he shocked me! And why not? Big Cáit was my brother Pádraig's wife, the mother of a flock of little children and a fine ball of a young woman. She was his second wife, as Máire Sheáin Bháin had lived only for a couple of years.

'What happened her?' I asked.

'She had a child and after the birth she made no battle.' he said.

'Where are you off to now?'

'To see would I find Pádraig. He and Máire'—that was my sister—'are gone off seeing about the order for the burial and the wake. The poor man is out of his mind with sorrow and no wonder he is.' With that he went off.

I had to sit down and cry. When my master returned to tackle the horse so as to go home he asked me what was wrong with me. When I told him what had happened he got very troubled.

'I won't be home with you at all,' I told him. 'I'll go to Dunquin but with God's help, I'll be back tomorrow after the funeral.'

'Very well,' he said.

I left him then and went off to join Seán and the others. I hadn't seen any of them for a year and a half previous to this and it was not a very pleasant time for a re-union. Each one of us felt nothing but sorrow and heartbreak. As regards Pádraig, the poor man was out of his mind.

We spent the evening busily gathering everything together and loading up the cart. By the time we had everything in order a fly wouldn't have found room in the vehicle. We propped up Old Séamaisín, the dead woman's father, between two boxes in some way or other as the poor man was unable to walk. There were no motor-cars in those days nor a single word about them, so Máire and Pádraig and myself had to use our legs. We had a mighty long road before us and by this time it was late enough in the evening. I thought of my unfortunate mother at home in a sad state indeed because trouble used knock her out completely. I knew that there was nothing to heal her—except perhaps the drop of whiskey which would deaden the dark thoughts running through

146

her mind. I went in and told the shopkeeper to give me a pint of whiskey; when he had it wrapped up in paper I hid it on my person and no one was the wiser.

When everything was ready Seán sat into the front of the cart and drove off the horse. We three moved after them. He was going at a nice steady pace because the horse was pulling a heavy load. It was getting late, and as I have already said, we had a **long** road before us— twelve miles west to Dunquin. Máire and I were well able for the road for we were hardy and strong, but poor Pádraig was like a half fool what with the drop of drink and the sorrow, so that we found it difficult to make him keep up with us. One minute he'd be crying and the next minute he'd be talking away and then, finally he'd, as it were, go on strike so as not to go home at all. But we kept coaxing him with us along the road.

Night had fallen, darkness had come down and the road before us was not too good—it was a deserted and difficult road and when we lost sight of the horse we could hear the noise of the cart and this gave us courage. We were coaxing Pádraig along all the while until we reached the Clasach Leacht. There the poor man was exhausted and down he fell in one dead heap. His face turned the colour of death.

'He's dead,' Máire said, 'what will we do now?'

Dear God, that was the time we really had the trouble because that was the loneliest part of the road. By this time a good portion of the night had gone by. What to do now—that was our problem. How could we leave Pádraig there? And neither of us, because of loneliness could remain with him while the other went off to look for help. We were in a right hobble! The dickens to it, if I didn't think of the bottle!

'Máire,' I said, 'I have a drop of whiskey and if we could only pour some of it back his throat . . .'

I took out the bottle but the cork was as firm in it as the handle is in a mallet and I had nothing with which to draw it at that time. The plan I thought of then was to knock the neck off the bottle between two stones. This done, I went over to where Máire was.

147

'Lift up his head,' I said. 'And be careful the glass doesn't cut him.'

She lifted up his head and I started pouring the drink back his throat, but more was spilled than went into his mouth. I rubbed the whiskey to his nose and to his lips and after a time he began to stir. I thought of the night that we had Micky in the same sad state in Dingle but the two cases weren't alike, for poor Pádraig was worn out from the road and the trouble, so that when the drink he had already taken died down in him, he couldn't endure any more. But I assure you, that before long he had recovered his senses and was walking lightly by our side.

Some of the boys had come out as far as Tobber to meet us because they thought that something had happened to delay us. When we came to Ballinglanna even the hardest-hearted person in the world would be moved by Pádraig's crying that night. What wonder was that? His fine young wife stretched out dead and a fleet of poor orphans around him; that was a hard circumstance for the unfortunate man to bear.

I made no great delay in the wake-house because the thought of my mother was troubling me. I still had the bottle in my pocket; the only cork I had was my finger stuck down into it because the paper around it had been carried away by the wind and I could get nothing else to serve as a cork.

As it was late at night I asked my father to go with me; when we came to Vicarstown my poor mother wasn't in very good heart before me but no matter!—she welcomed me. I gave her a sup out of the bottle since there was no better doctor to give her a helping hand at that moment than the whiskey. This I knew well and I didn't spare it on her. My father drank a drop too; the poor man needed it also. I assure you, dear reader, that before long the old woman was sleeping soundly! I don't know what time she woke because when it brightened for day I went off to Ballinglanna.

As soon as ever the funeral was over I walked away east along the road and I never stopped until I reached my master's house. The woman of the house had welcome

148

for me because she never expected me to return so soon. The neighbours gathered in and sympathized with me on the death of my brother's wife; but as the proverb has it, 'There's no cure for misfortune but to kill it with patience!'

A fortnight before Christmas I got a letter from my old friend, Cáit-Jim, telling me to get ready, that she had decided to send me the passage-money for St. Patrick's Day. My dear man, my heart was filled with joy. I'd now be free from the power of slavery and I'd be independent of everyone.

The woman of the house asked me who the letter was from: I told her that it had come from a dear friend who was going to send me my passage-money to America. 'I'll be going home after Christmas,' I added.

By the Lord, but she scowled! That same didn't cost me a thought.

Match and Marriage

*Cáit-Jim's letter — How a match was made for me — A
wedding and a wake together — My first trip on the sea —
The Island and the second wedding-feast*

WHEN Christmas was over I collected my belongings and
bade my employers farewell; to be quite candid I wasn't
very upset about leaving, for believe you me, I ate little
idle bread while I was under that roof.

Aye, I was back home again and I was on tenterhooks
waiting for another letter from Cáit-Jim. But, alas, when
it came, it disappointed me sorely because it told me that
she could not send me the money this time for she had
injured her hand and could do no work. So she had no
relief to offer me.

I got really downhearted but there was nothing for it
but to make the best of the story. I gave no one the
slightest information on the subject and I never pretended
that I had heard other than the best possible news.

One Saturday in the beginning of Shrove, Seán was in
Dingle; when he came home he told me that he had
news for me.

'What news?' I asked him.

'News of a match, my girl!'

'God above! Who's the man?'

'An Islandman,' he said. 'An even-tempered, honest
boy and a good man as well, so I hope you'll take my
advice. They'll be coming to visit us some night soon.'

The way matters then stood between my brother Seán
and myself, if he ordered me to go and bail the ocean I'd
obey him for no one in the world stood higher in my
affections than did Seán.

150

Three nights after this, three men walked in the door. They got a hearty welcome. My father had no idea that they were coming but then he realized fully what had brought them. After a little while one of the men produced from his pocket a bottle with a long neck; bottle followed bottle until they had a fair share of drink taken and then we had no shortage of talk! I didn't open my mouth, but I was peeping from under my eyelashes at the young men. I couldn't decide which of the three was asking for me because I knew none of them. I could neither choose one nor bar any. Each one of them was too good a man for me even if I were seven times a better woman than I was.

Oh dear, that match didn't take long to make! There was little more to it than 'Come along' and 'I'm satisfied.' My father came over to me.

'Raise up your head!' he said. 'Will you go to the Island?'

I considered for a while for I had two choices in the palm of my hand—to marry or go into service again. I was sick and tired of that same service and I thought it would be better for me to have a man to my back and someone to protect me, and to own a house too, where I could sit down at my ease whenever I'd be weary.

My father spoke again: 'What have you to say?' he asked.

'I know nothing at all about the Island people,' I said, 'but you know them through and through. Whatever pleases you pleases me and I'll go wherever you tell me.'

'God be with you,' my father said.

The bargain was made; Peats Guiheen and myself were to be married in a few days' time.

Saturday was the day appointed. There were neither motor-cars nor side-cars there at that time—it's a different story altogether nowadays. When we were ready that morning Seán tackled the horse and a crowd of us sat into the cart. When we got to Ballyferriter, the place was black with people for there were seven weddings there that day and there was a great throng of people present.

When we left the chapel there was right tip-of-the-reel

151

and hullabaloo; the young people had music and dancing and the older people were singing and drinking. A good part of the day was spent like this; when Seán called for me it was time for everyone to be moving towards the house, so some other girls and myself went off home with him. It was customary at that time for everyone who attended the ceremony to go to the house for the wedding reception. The men would arrive later in ones until at last we were all together. Then the revelry would begin.

But when we got home there was no good news to greet us but word that a fine big daughter of my brother Seán was at death's door. We never expected news like that for the fit had come on her all of a sudden. She died that same night.

So, according as each man arrived at the house he'd sit down quietly without speaking a word. Ever afterwards my brother had great affection for the Island people because of the fine manner in which they had sympathized with him that night.

We had a wedding-feast and a wake at one and the same time. That's the way my poor wedding went.

The Islanders had decided to go home on the following Tuesday. Seán tackled the horse; then two barrels of porter, a jar of whiskey and the eatables that hadn't been consumed because of the girl's death, were loaded onto the cart. Then we moved off down to Barra na hAille —the cliff top. My sister Máire was with me, as was Cáit, my brother's wife. When we reached the creek four currachs were launched on the water and the barrels and other goods were loaded into one. There were four men to each currach. I sat into the stern of the currach in which my husband was and as this was my first time ever on the sea I was terrified out of my wits.

The evening was beautiful and the sea was calm and the men were rowing easily until at last we reached the Island haven. I was as amazed that evening as if I were entering the city of London. When we moved close to the Island the place was black with people big and small all gathered there to welcome us. I made my way through the crowds as best I could and all the while I was turning over in my mind how I'd come to accept this kind of home without a relation or a friend near me. I didn't know one person among all those who were shaking hands with me and I kept asking myself if the day would ever dawn when I'd open my heart to these people or make as bold among them as I would among the people of Vicarstown. Oh, never, never, I told myself, could they be as kind as the people of Vicarstown. The blessing of God be with you, Cáit-Jim, I said in my own mind, you were the lucky one! Whatever happens, your feet will be planted on mainland clay. Not so with me! How lonely I am on this island in the ocean with nothing to be heard forever more but the thunder of the waves hurling themselves on the beach. But I have one consolation—a fine handsome man, and as I can gather from the whispering going on around me I'm not the first woman who cocked her cap at him! But he's mine now, and no thanks to them to do without him! I'll have friends aplenty on this Island as long as God leaves him to me. And hasn't he a fine presentable appearance! And his knowledge of the ways of the sea! I thought I would never be in danger of drowning if he and I were in the same currach.

I stayed where I was until my husband came to me and then, side by side, we walked upwards to the house with a crowd of the village children following us. They were wild for sweets, the poor things, and their mouths were working at the thoughts of them.

The old people of the place had gathered into the house to welcome me. I was shy and backward because I knew none of them, but before long I pulled myself together. Then Old Mící Guiheen, my father-in-law, addressed me; he was a rough strong hardy man but age was catching up on him. 'Flint' was his nickname.

'Welcome a hundred thousand times, Peig,' he said.

'That you may live long in the whole of your health,' I answered and my head was bent with a sort of shyness.

'Take your shawl and hang it up there, child,' said Máire O'Sullivan, my mother-in-law. She was, as the saying goes, all about me! Then: 'Never mind! I'll do it myself as you're exhausted,' she added.

I took off my shawl and she hung it on a little peg that was driven into the wall. You're a good mother-in-law and a gentle one too, I told myself, and it's a great blessing that I took the sound advice of my brother Seán. I knew well that Seán didn't want to tie me to a good-for-nothing, so I didn't go against him the night my match was being made.

Peats Flint was now bound to me by the Church; we belonged to each other and everything we owned we held in common. That was the way we promised it would be. Many a person promises and is sorry afterwards, but I wasn't sorry when I saw these fine people-in-law around me. They had the house very nicely and tastefully done up, the walls bright with whitewash, new furniture too, and gleaming sand spread on the hearth. A neat lamp hung by the side of the wall and the dresser was laden with lovely delf. A great grey cat with a gloss on its fur lay in the corner; there was also a small dog—the little fellow came to make friends with me and lay down beside me. My husband Peats and his brother, Mícheál, were busy about the house putting things to rights, for the local people were due to arrive as soon as ever the lights were lighting, for the wedding celebrations had not yet ended.

We hadn't the tea finished when a crowd of old women gathered in, Cáit O'Brien the weaver's wife, then Molleen and Máire Kearney, Nell Keane, and Cáit Mhór. This same Cáit O'Brien was a great person to make sport, may God have mercy on her soul for she too has passed over as indeed they all have. And may all their souls be at peace.

When we had the tea drank Peats Flint got up and brought out a bottle of whiskey. Removing the cork he gave a good glass to each one present. I tell you, dear reader, that the old women showered blessings on us! Later still, Peats with two others from the neighbourhood went down to the creek, taking with them two currach masts with which to bring back the barrels of porter that were below. Two barrels meant four men to bring the load back to the house and Peats had no shortage of help, I assure you, for the men were clipping the heels of each other in their hurry, one man arriving with a hemp rope and two others following with the two currach masts on their shoulders. Such running and racing I never saw before! In a moment they had made a sort of a hand-barrow out of the masts and the rope. 'That will do the job now, Peats,' says Peats Tom Kearney.

'You think it will? Is every knot on the one draw?'

'Aye, indeed. Have no fear; there's no danger that any knot will slip.'

'That's the way they'll have to be,' said Peats, 'because a barrel of porter is mighty weighty, you must realize.'

When they were gone down by the corner of Eoin's garden Máire O'Sullivan rose from the stool and proceeded down into the room. Nobody knew what she was up to until she walked haughtily back up the floor with the bottle in her hand.

'I'd swear, Máire,' said Cáit Mhór, 'that there's nothing good on your mind!'

'Not at all, Cáit Mhór; it's my own child's share and little more you'll get this night when the crowd'll gather in.' Then she added, 'And if I wanted anything in the morning 'tis you I'd face because you never begrudged me anything.'

'Be easy now, Máire, a thimbleful will do me,' said Cáit O'Brien.

'It will not do you, Cáit! There's more where this bottle came from,' Máire said.

'Drink it, Cáit,' I put in.

'Wisha, Peigí, I won't refuse you. But upon my soul it isn't with mind for it I'm drinking it.'

Everyone drank a little share and you can rest assured that we had talk and conversation, for many's the subject was discussed that evening by the fireside.

When Peats and the others came back with the barrels the people started to crowd in. I had no idea that there were so many people on the Island and soon the little house was thronged. There was only a rectangular patch in the middle of the floor that no one liked to stand on; outside of that the people were crushing each other and bobbing up and down behind one another's backs.

The girls and boys there were handsome, pleasant and kind. My heart was lively that night as I watched them raising dust from the floor as they yielded to the gentle merry music of the violin—lashings of drink too, as from time to time, a white bucket with snow-white foam on its top did the rounds of the house. Here and there among the people a man raised his own ditty and everyone was merry and happy as the night slipped by. If we hadn't a wedding feast on the mainland we had one on the Island. When the drink began to work Micil—he was an uncle to my husband—no one outdid him at singing from ten o'clock at night until six in the morning. Micil was a very fine singer indeed and a man of great heart on sea and on land. You wouldn't feel a long summer's day passing in his company.

The young people too had capering, dancing and music—all this until it was time to go home.

A New and Different World

I experience a new world — Neighbouring women around me — The Islandman at the mill — I make new friends — On the Island hill — Learning to keep house

THE following day my sister Máire took leave of us and she and the others went off home. I was sort of lonely after them but the feeling of loneliness didn't last very long because I had plenty of company. There is always company on the Island.

At last I had a house of my own and I could sit down and get up whenever I pleased. Not a bitter word was uttered towards me and I had a quiet, sensible man to look after me—one who'd allow no one to sneer at me— a change indeed from the time when I was at the mercy of strangers. A new life, as I have already said, with my own home and my own affairs to look after. The days of my youth were certainly gone forever and I had to spend the balance of my life in ease or in hardship according as they came my road.

But alas and alas, it was a troubled and tormented life that lay in store for me, as I shall set down hereafter. But as yet there wasn't a single cloud to mar the sky of my life. I had nothing to bother me in those days but companionship and sport and those things I had in plenty, since you can take it from me that there was delightful company on the Island at that time with a crowd of sprightly lads and well-brought-up mannerly girls. That's how they were then and that's how they are to this day although there are many who imagine that the Island people are wild and that they should have horns growing out of their heads.

Let me tell you what happened to an Islandman on one occasion many years ago. He passed east through Dingle on his way to the pounding-mill with two bags of wool to be carded. There was a crowd of women at the mill before him and the miller told them that they'd have to allow the Islandman go first because he had travelled such a long journey from home. *Erra*, man dear, when they heard that he was from the Great Blasket Island they were staring at him so intently that you'd think they would eat him up with their eyes. The miller noticed them.

'The devil fire ye!' he said. 'What staring have ye at that decent man? Can't ye see that he's as gentle, as kind and as capable-looking as any other man? Or is it the way ye think he has horns growing out of his head?'

When they heard this they shrivelled up, and even if he had six horns on his head they wouldn't have dared to look at him any more. That same man was the handsomest and nicest man on the Island, God be good to his soul. The people in this Island are pleasant, honest, generous and hospitable and the stranger can experience friendship and kindness among them. And if he doesn't, it's his own fault!

A few mornings after I got married, as I was out at the little well beside the house drawing a bucket of water, who came towards me across the Road of the Dead but Cáit O'Brien.

'God bless you this morning,' she said. 'Isn't it early you're at your work?'

'I don't usually sleep out late in the morning, Cáit,' I told her. 'Before ever I came here I ate no easy bread.'

'I know that, child,' she said. 'That's how matters stand with anyone who spends his life bound to others.'

'The dickens take it, Cáit!' I said. 'I'm thinking now that some people have to live far away from home. A couple of days ago I got a letter from my friend, Cáit-Jim, who's in America and the news I read in that letter gave me little pleasure. She told me that she couldn't send me my fare, and I was sorely disappointed.'

'You had your mind made up to go to America, so?'

'You can say that again! But I had to give over the idea then. After that I decided to go in service once more but that same eluded me too!'

'Never mind, Peigí! Marriage was laid out for you.'

'I don't know on earth, Cáit O'Brien,' I said. 'I think this is a very confined place with the sea out there to terrorize me. And it's out on that sea my husband will spend half his life from this day forward.'

'That's the run of life here, child, and you'll have to put up with it. But you won't have a whole lot to do unless you prefer it otherwise. You have a good mother-in-law and three nice sisters-in-law living in the house with you and it's quite easy for you to meet your equal on this Island—that I assure you. There's Nell Keane back here in the west, she's only a couple of months married too.'

'But Nell Keane is used to the Island and she has her mother and father at her side if she needs them. If my father and mother were here too I wouldn't be half as much in dread. But they are beyond my call.'

'You're right there, Peigí. You'd be a whole lot braver if they were here, but pay no heed to it. If anything is bothering you what's to stop you from going out to Dunquin to your own people's house and staying there until everything is right?

'But as regards the ocean,' she went on, 'don't be one bit worried. Peats, your husband, is a very skilled man and there's no end to his knowledge of the ways of the sea. I hear my own people saying that a man as good as him never gripped the two oars of a currach except alone Seán Eoin and Peats Mhicí. Did you ever hear the song of praise that Seán Dunlea made up about them when they won the currach race in Ventry? Young Mícheál Keane was fourth man in the currach that day, God rest his soul!

'I tell you, Peigí, and believe it from me too,' she continued, 'many a person has fared worse than you. Pull yourself together and let's go in. The air is sharp and it's cold out here under the sky. I came over to tell Máire O'Sullivan that Eoghan has the piece of flannel finished. Máire is an old friend of mine and it shortens my day

159

greatly to spend a while in her company. Eoghan, my own man, tells me that he prefers Máire even to any one of his own sisters! Eoghan is a great man for fun and enjoyment and if you were interested in hearing himself and Máire O'Sullivan telling of the life they lived in days gone by, you'd travel a long road to listen to them.'

'I'll visit you from this out, Cáit,' I told her.

'And you'll be welcome, darling. And Eoghan himself will be delighted that you're coming. Fill up that bucket now and let's be off in.'

My mother-in-law was sitting in the corner turning the wool-spinning wheel. 'Sit here!' she told me, 'and card a handful of these rolls of wool for me.'

'Just as well for her to get used to the work because she won't have you always!' Cáit O'Brien remarked.

'She won't have me, woman dear,' Máire said, 'for with every day that passes we're moving towards the grave.'

'I heard Siobhán was thinking of pulling out and going off to America,' Cáit O'Brien went on.

'She is, and her sister, Cáit, will be off with her. They'd rather do that than put down roots here. But one thing is certain, Cáit O'Brien, and I'm talking privately to a woman I trust, I'll die with sorrow when they're gone for my heart is wrapped up in them.'

'No wonder you would, my poor woman! When our own Peig went away I went close to being found demented in Glenagalt—the glen of the mad. But see how I became reconciled!'

'It wasn't easy!'

'It was hard, indeed. There's no harder fate except death than looking at your own child after your life spent rearing her, being snapped out of your two hands. No word of a lie, Máire, I gave fifteen days crying and pining after Peig had left. But from that day out I wasn't as lonely after any other member of the family.'

'Am I doing all right?' I asked, breaking in on her conversation, for I wasn't used to that kind of work.

'Sure, you are,' Cáit answered. 'I don't think you'll need much teaching.' Then she stirred herself to go.

'Are you off, Cáit?' Máire asked.

'Aye! I came to tell you that the weaver has the piece of flannel finished.'

'Very well! I'll go west at nightfall.'

'Don't forget to bring Peig with you.'

'Nothing to stop her if she wants to go.'

When she had **gone** I told Máire that I'd like to go because Cáit O'Brien **was** the first woman on the Island in whom I had confided.

'Poor Cáit is good. And she has another virtue too, for she isn't loose-tongued like a lot more. You could tell her a secret that would hang you if it was known.'

When night fell we went across the quarry where Micí Dhiarmada saw the ghost and then down by the Road of the Dead. There we turned up to the right and again we turned at the corner of the White Field and went on until we reached Eoghan O'Connor's, the weaver's.

When Eoghan saw me he got up from the chair and shook hands with me. 'A hundred thousand welcomes here,' he said, 'daughter of a good mother—and of a good father too. Often he and I had a drink together in Dingle and he's a gentle quiet man and a noted story-teller as well.'

He asked me many questions about my own people and I did my best to answer them. When we were on the point of coming home Cáit O'Brien insisted on my drinking a cup of tea with her, and she wouldn't take no for an answer. From that day until the day she died she was a dear friend of mine.

The first thing I did the following morning was to go to the hill. The day was very fine and the devil picked me until I got this mad desire to go on the hill for a load of turf, so that in the end nothing would satisfy me but to see the hill of the Island. Flint tackled the donkey for me and I moved upwards humming away to myself as I went. As luck would have it who was going up that same day but Cáit O'Brien. She was still hardy and strong and my word, I was delighted to have her company. She waited for me above on top of the causeway, a short distance up from the houses. We were walking along side by side until we reached the crest of the road.

'As I love God, Cáit,' I said, 'isn't this a queer place? How is it that the cows don't fall over the edge of the cliff? Is the Island all as high as this? I'm shivering in my skin with dread when I look down on the blue sea running right underneath me and then when I look up I see a hill-top between me and the sky. Is it the same as this from here back to Black Head?'

'I own to God, child, but it's more or less the same. But when we reach Builteán the going will be easier. I thought the same way as you have just now described the first day I came on the hill with old Nell O'Connor. She was laughing at me, so one day yet, you'll wonder, Peig, —that is if you have a long life here—how everything on the Island once held such interest for you. Come to think of it, I was worse than you! After my five years in the great town of Tralee I wasn't slow to marry Eoghan Bán and come to the Island with him. Needless to say, ever since then, he never left me hungry nor thirsty and you'll have the same story, with God's help. You have a good man and you need never be afraid that he'll insult you either.'

I laughed a little and then said: 'It eases my mind to hear everyone praising him.'

'He's worth it!' Cáit said. 'God leave him to you and God leave everyone his own share as well.'

At long last we came to the bog, which was an almost flat-topped mound overgrown with fine attractive heather. From this hillock I had a view of Inishvickillane and Inishnabro.

'Aren't those islands lovely?' I said, thinking at the same time that I'd like to go west to visit them in a currach on a fine day.

'It looks as if they are,' Cáit answered. 'On your feet now and load up your donkey! You needn't go any further to the west for our rick of turf will serve today. We'll go west for a load another day.'

'That's just as handy for me,' I said. 'That way we'll be home together again.'

We came to our feet and it didn't take us long to fill our loads. When I returned home, Micí told me to untackle the ass.

'*Sha*,' said Máire O'Sullivan when I went in, 'how did you like the hill?'

'I liked it well,' I replied. 'It's very beautiful, but Cáit O'Brien will tell you the whole story when she comes visiting in the evening.'

The Birth of My First Child

A visit to my old home — My mother's anxiety — I give birth to a son — 'Who is he like?'

CÁIT O'Brien never spoke a truer word than when she told me that I wouldn't have to do a hand's turn unless I wished it. I had a good woman beside me on my floor and three pleasant girls who never said as much as 'Watch out!' to me until eventually they left the house; to tell the truth I was lonely after them when they hoisted their sails and went away. Siobhán and Cáit were the first to go. Peig stayed at home; she married an O'Donnell man in the parish of 'Ferriter.

Yes, life was moving along slowly and deliberately like the movements of a clock and my time was drawing near. The dark cloud was casting its shadow over me again. What would I do—stay on the Island for the birth of the child or go home to my father's and mother's house until everything was over and done with? I asked my mother-in-law's advice; she took my view of things at once, and said that going home was a good idea. Then she added:

'If you need a priest or a doctor there will be a dry road to travel, and indeed, my dear girl, we have little means to back us here. Another thing, your mind will be more at ease when you're with your own mother for there's nothing wrong with you except the feeling of loneliness we all have experienced when we were the way you are now. In God's name get yourself ready in the morning and go off out home to your mother. From the very moment you realize that that is what you'd prefer to do, then do it and probably it's for your welfare. We'll carry on as best

164

we can until you come back, with the help of God. *Sha,* be easy in your mind now! God is good from one day until the next.'

The following morning Peats, my husband, got ready and called two other neighbours. The poor fellows— there wasn't a lazy bone in their bodies; they hadn't to be called a second time—they came willingly.

We made our way down to the creek. When Cáit O'Brien heard that I was going away she came with me to the water's edge.

'God bring ye safely across the sea,' she said, 'and may the Lord bring us the best of news.'

'Amen!' I said in a low voice.

The currach was launched and we moved out. Even though the day was fine there was a sweeping swell in the creek but nevertheless the men kept manoeuvring the currach until there was a calm interval. When they got the lull they sped away and then it was glorious.

When we were some distance out to sea what rounded the Point but a great ship. That was the first day ever I was close to a steamship; it moved within scraping distance of us and if I had known the crew I could have recognized every one of them—the vessel was so near us. She passed us by, cleaving the waves on either side and the small white eddies in her wake almost spilled into the currach. Numerous sea birds flew about us—this because there was a great amount of food moving past us from the north with the flow of the tide.

I was facing for my native townland again but this journey was unlike any other journey I had ever made before. I wondered if the wrangling still went on between them at home or if Cáit, my brother's wife, now ruled the roost. If that was the case, it was a certainty that the angel of peace would walk among them! Whether or no we would have to go there now.

When we moved in towards the Great Cliff the water was as calm as a lake. Then we travelled eastwards through the parish and Peats came with me to Vicarstown.

Erra, man alive, it wasn't the same house at all! I never thought I'd see Cáit as pleasant as she was for she almost pulled me asunder with sheer affection. I knew at once what had happened.

'Thank God,' I said in my own mind, 'the dispute is over. The sallow lass has won the race and she's boss at last. I'll get no rasp of her tongue now—as I often got of old!'

My mother got a fit of joyful crying when she saw me. 'What's wrong?' she asked finally when the little spasm of grief had passed. I barely understood what she was saying, her voice was so weak.

'Not a thing, Mom, thanks be to God,' I said. 'We're well pleased with the way things are going, but I decided to come here because my time has almost come and I thought you'd be the best to look after me.'

'Is that it, child?' she said. 'I thought at first that something else had brought ye and then again since I'm not as well as I'd like to be, I surely got a start. Certainly it's here with us you'll get the best attention for the time being.'

During this time Cáit was busy making tea for us and when we had the tea drank Peats said that he'd go home —that is if it was all right with me.

'Just as well for you, my man,' my mother said. 'You'll get word, for maybe events mightn't happen as soon as you expect. A boat will be going in and out every day from this forward and we'll send you news. Don't fret in the slightest on her account for she'll be fine, with the help of God.'

Himself and my brother Seán then went west to the cliff-top.

Three days after Peats had left me, I gave birth to a young son. Believe you me, dear reader, that little stranger was welcome. When Nell Pheig, the midwife, handed me the child I couldn't describe my joy. We had a little celebration that night and I can tell you that Nell Pheig was marvellous company.

The following morning who should walk in the door but my husband Peats—and no one expecting him!

'Aye!' said my mother. 'Herself is fine, thank God. She has a young son since just before daybreak.'

'That's good news and God be thanked,' he said. Then: 'Where's the child?' Nell brought him the infant.

'Who is he like?' he said, taking the child smartly and kissing it.

'I own to God!' he said. 'He isn't like me at all but he's the dead spit of her brother Seán. He has the same cocked-up nose on him!'

'Peats,' I said, 'that same wouldn't be a fault on the child.'

'I'm not saying that at all, my darling woman. He'd be taking after a good man if he took after Seán.'

We had a gay day and the following morning the child was brought to Ballyferriter to be baptized. The Parish Priest at that time was Father Seán O'Leary.

I was asked that morning what name I'd like to call the infant and I told them I'd prefer to have him called Seán. But Peats said that he'd rather call him Muiris because Muiris was the name of his brother who had gone to America many years before.

'I won't break your word,' I said. 'Call him whatever name you like!'

We had a night and a half when they returned from Ballyferriter. 'Twas like a little wedding and I promise you that old Nell Pheig wasn't thirsty! She was a low-sized, tidy, blooming woman and she had the reputation of having cures. At any rate, the whiskey wasn't spared on her. I don't think there was another household in the parish of Dunquin as gay as we were that night.

My Life on the Island

I return to the Island — How the two old men saw two moons in the sky

AFTER I had spent six weeks in Vicarstown I thought it time to return home; the best part of my story was that myself and my child were returning well and happy.

Sunday was the day I had decided upon to return. Peats, his brother Mícheál, and two others came for me from the Island in a currach. When we were ready to leave my mother spoke up from the corner.

'Bring me the infant,' she said, 'until I bid him my last good-bye!'

She took the child in her arms and kissed him lovingly and tenderly.

'May God make you a fine big man some day, my little one,' she said. 'Good-bye now and my blessing go with you to the Island. I shall never see you again.' She didn't either, for she died soon afterwards.

She held out the child to me and said: 'May you prosper by the hand of everyone and by my hand too.' Then we set off.

The evening was delightful; the ocean was calm and it didn't take us long to get home. I can tell you, dear reader, that that was the happiest and most heartwarming day I have ever spent before or since.

When we reached the landing-slip, my old friend, Cáit O'Brien, and Máire Kearney, and even old Máire O'Sullivan herself, were before me on the shore. Máire O'Sullivan snatched the child away as an eagle snatches a young lamb. The poor old woman was beside herself with glee.

'My suckling dearie! My little white angel!' she kept repeating.

168

Cáit O'Brien stayed with me and accompanied me to the house. There was a good number of the old women inside before me; that's a custom old women have everywhere and one to which the old Islandwomen weren't immune.

Each one delivered her own summing-up on the child. According to one, he had this fault and that fault: the nose was a little too big, the eyes were small, the ears weren't exactly perfect and so on. At last the grandfather, Mící, who had been sitting by the fire raised his voice.

'May blindness and shortsightedness overtake ye!' he said. ''Tis hard for anyone to have a flaw unknown to ye. And all that peering ye have at the child! Doesn't youth go through many a change!'

'True, indeed,' said Cáit O'Brien in reply. 'But I daresay everyone takes a lot of notice of the first child.'

'My word!' Mící answered. 'It's all the same whether it's the first child or the last. Often it's 'the scraping of the skillet' is the one you'd like the most.'

'With that I agree!' said Máire Kearney stirring herself on the stool. 'The last child might matter most to you; indeed 'tis often an unfortunate woman reared a fine clutch of a family and the last child of all would turn out to be the best head to her.'

'That often happened!' Mící said. 'But forget it for a story and make the tea.'

Before long the old woman began to scatter and then the only one left was Cáit O'Brien.

'You ran 'em, Mící!' she said.

'You know well, Cáit,' Mící replied, 'that God's Paradise won't be in the better of having those women inside its gates for it won't take them twenty-four hours to upset heaven.'

'I declare to God, Mící, you're dead right. It's as well for me to be moving off to the east. The dickens, but Eoghan will give me a bar of the tongue.'

'*Erra*, woman, aren't you in a hurry! Wait and drink a cup of tea with us.'

'My insides are scalded from it, Mící! But as the tea is going just now I'll drink a cup out of my hand and eat a bite of shop-bread.'

At this time of my life, dear reader, I had the world and all of contrairy things to attend to. Now and again I had to mind the child, but that was very seldom indeed for I had a·prime nurse minding him as long as his grandmother lived. Often when I'd be on my road home from the hill with a load of turf I'd hear her from the top of Tóchar singing for the child.

'Wisha,' she would say:

Muirisín's your name and Muirisín's your uncle
And Muirisín you've been to the seventh generation.
March to the doorway and back to the chimney nook
And I'll warm your shins if you're slow at ambulation.

At this time everything was plentiful on the Island. What with the harvest of the sea the people had sufficient food of their own. Every house had a cow and many houses had two cows. The young people were marrying and settling down; at the time I speak of, fourteen cradles rocked infants on the Island—this although the young people going nowadays don't even know what a cradle is! An Island marriage at that time was like a banquet; you've heard the expression 'They had a wedding celebration that lasted for seven days and seven nights.' In the same way perhaps four days after a wedding here you'd find an old fellow in an odd corner piping up with *Dónal na Gréine* and his wits completely astray.

A couple of years after my own marriage, Pádraig Keane and Bríghdín O'Shea got married. There was a great deal of food and drink at the wedding; shop bread and jam were novelties in those days and those two commodities were there in plenty. Lots of porter and whiskey too! The couple were connected with us so everyone in the house attended the wedding except myself and the old man. I was put out at not being able to go, but I had no way out of it because the child was too young and I had to remain at home to mind him. Just the same I had company, for old Muiris from Barrawalla and Peaidí

170

Ruadh came in the door. The old man welcomed them for they were his own cronies.

'Why aren't you at the wedding, Muiris?' he enquired.

'Indeed I am not,' Muiris answered, 'for I was thinking that you were here all by yourself!'

'I was, too,' the old man said.

They were chatting away and discussing life in general for a while and before long the newly-married man arrived with a bucket of porter and a narrow-necked bottle of whiskey the length of your arm.

'Take that in your hand, Micí, and drink my health!' he said.

'Indeed I will and welcome,' said Micí.

I had to get drinking glasses for the bridegroom and he started doling out the whiskey. When Pádraig Keane had spent a while with us he wanted to go back to where the company was, so he got up off the chair.

'Be chatting away and drinking now,' he said, 'for maybe ye'll never attend another wedding in your lives.' Away with him then.

Then the talk and the foolish prattle began. The old men were recounting their deeds and bragging of their prowess and heroism in their younger days so that we never felt the night slipping by. At last Muiris got up and walked to the doorway and I daresay that by this time his eyes weren't too good. The night was bright for the moon was shining brightly in the sky.

'I declare to my God!' he said looking up in amazement, 'I've seen something tonight that I never saw before.'

'What is it you see?' said Peaidí.

'There are two moons in the sky this night,' he said.

'Raving you are, my man!' said Peaidí.

'No, no, I assure you,' said Muiris. 'Come to the door and I bet you'll see them yourself.'

The pair of them went to the door.

'God grant it to my soul, but he's right! Micí, could you ever hoist yourself up? I never saw anything like this since the day I was christened Pádraig Ruadh!'

'Before God!' said Micí, 'there must be something

dreadful outside.' He caught his walking stick and down he went but alas! there was nothing to be seen but a single moon hanging brilliantly in the air.

'Sit above there in the chair for yourself, Muiris,' Mící said. 'Your wits are scattered to God and the world. Maybe it's dead in the glen you'll be found by morning.'

'My! but you're absolutely right!' Muiris said. 'Being here is the same as being at home!'

He sat on the chair and before long all three of them were in a stupor of sound sleep. I fell asleep myself too.

The child crying in the cradle woke me. It was broad daylight. The others had slept off their drunkenness so they all went home.

Comfort and Grief

My children grow up — Siobhán dies — A scrap of comfort for me

ONE year good and another bad, that's the way my life went by, and as the years passed I became fully convinced that a harsh life lay in store for me and that I'd have to harden myself so as to prepare for it. Each year brought its own changes: to one person it brought comfort, to another affliction: then the year would slip by just as the tide ebbs from the sand of the beach.

I was pulling away through life pretty easily as yet, with my family increasing as one child followed another. But then poor Máire, my husband's mother, died, peace be to her soul, and her death dealt me a severe blow. But before she died she passed on to me every item of knowledge so that she had made me a competent housewife; she taught me how to spin and knit and to do everything that had to do with household duties.

When poor Máire died I had the house to myself except for Mici who lived on for a few years after her. The children were growing up; six of them lived—two girls, Cáit and Eibhlín, and four boys, Muiris, Pádraig, Mícheál and Tomás. The lads were forever watching out for their father whenever he'd return from the sea. If he happened to catch some unusual little fish they'd wrangle with each other to see who would have it.

'Wisha, children,' he'd say, 'isn't it all the same which of ye gets it? Aren't ye all the one?'

But that wouldn't solve it; often I had to get up from the spinning-wheel and get the rod to separate them.

Their father got great amusement out of watching them disputing with each other. You'd know by the way he eyed them that he had the height of affection for them.

173

The poor man was labouring away as best as he possibly could to push them ahead in the world. He never returned home to them empty-handed; he always had some mouthful or other and we'd make the best of it. But the night he'd be out fishing for mackerel I wouldn't close an eye! Dear reader, I was terrified! I'd have my ear cocked until I'd hear him coming and many's the long night I spent by the fireside until day dawned without a single spark of courage in my heart. Muiris and Cáit, the two eldest of the family, would sit up with me. When the night was well advanced Muiris would say:

174

'I don't know what's keeping Daidí. Seldom would he be out so long.'

'Darling child, I don't know,' I'd answer. 'Likely they came across a share of fish. They'll be here shortly.'

'Indeed,' Cáit would say, 'I don't like my father being a fisherman. I'd prefer if he had any other sort of a living. Muiris,' she would add, 'we should think of him ever and always.'

'And won't we too, Cáitín? When we'll be grown up Daidí won't have to do a stroke of work.'

'Fine talk, children!' I'd say. 'Many a lifetime will be over and done with before ye'll be able to work for your father. But it's a great thing to have hopes of it anyway.'

'Don't say that, Maimí,' Cáit would say, standing up and stretching herself up. 'Amn't I a big woman already?'

With that there is a sound on the door. Cáit, her face as white as the wall, runs and crouches in fright between me and the hob.

'Aren't you the bad soldier?' I say.

'Who's out, Mom?'

'Daidí, child! Who else can it be?'

Muiris comes quickly to his feet and opens the door. Peats comes in with a hank of mackerel on a string.

'Bless my soul, Daidí, didn't it take you a long time to come home to me?'

'We filled the canoe tonight. I'm just back from Crooked Creek.'

'Ye won't go out again tonight?'

'We won't,' he'd maybe say. 'It's almost brightening for day now. It's a great shame for you not to go to sleep for yourself.'

'Sleep is it? Man dear, don't dream of mentioning sleep or rest to me while you're out fishing!'

But God help me, it wasn't long after that until I had to do without him altogether.

While the children were growing up the school wasn't a stone's throw away from them and I was easy in my mind while they were attending school. I was terrified they'd be drowned on the beach because they were obsessed

175

with the notion of going there when they were small. The breed of the sea was in them. Often I'd smash their toy boats. Then again, while they were attending school they could have little recourse to the strand for when they'd come home from school I'd put them drawing turf and at night they'd have their lessons to occupy their minds. Scarcely an evening passed without Cáit O'Brien paying us a visit.

You can well understand that at that time poor people weren't too hot in their skins. Potatoes and fish was their fare with now and again an odd mouthful of meat—good wholesome food—that's what they had at that time. At certain times of the year there was milk but, my word, it's often we had to do with very little of that same. The children grew up and, thanks be to God, they never went to bed hungry. They were cross enough when they were small but then again, sense never comes before age. But alas and alas, death gored us! It swept three of my family in their infancy and then measles took Siobhán, a fine bouncer of a girl eight years old.

But no one in this life is exempt from the law of God and it gives me pleasure to think that they are before me in the Kingdom of Heaven and my prayer is that the God of Glory will grant myself and those of my children still alive never to break His law in this life in such a way as would separate us on Judgement Day, but that my little family will rise up from the dead about me and that we'll all be united in the Kingdom of God.

Well! I had buried four of my children and, worse still, their father's health was broken for he caught a cold out fishing and he was making no headway towards recovery.

One day, I had buried my fourth child and it was no wonder that I was troubled in my mind. As the evening was fine I decided to go out so I took up a stocking from the window in order to be knitting, but to tell you the truth, I hadn't much mind for work that same evening. I drove the cow back before me and let her into the field for I reckoned that I could do no better than sit down for a while herding her.

I sat on the bank above the beach where I had a splendid view all around me. Dead indeed is the heart from which the balmy air of the sea cannot banish sorrow and grief. The passage between the Great Blasket and Beginnis is like a little harbour and it looks most attractive when the weather is calm. As I had no interest in the work I put down my stocking on a tussock and began to look away out to sea at the thousands of seabirds flying here and there in search of a bite to eat. Every bird from the stormy petrel to the cormorant, from the sand-snipe to the gannet was there and each variety of bird had its own peculiar call. There were many thousands of small seagulls; some, hovering lightly, were searching for little sprat or other morsels of food. Whenever one of them found a mouthful she'd utter a call and straightaway thousands of others were down on top of her. Such scuffling and pecking no one ever saw before! They were all entangled in one another trying to snatch the morsel from her.

At last I grew tired of watching the gulls and I turned my gaze to the south—towards Iveragh and Dingle Bay. It was a beautiful view. The whole bay was as calm as new milk, with little silver spray shimmering on its surface under a sunlight that was then brilliant. To the south Slea Head stood boldly in view as if it would stand there for ever—not a stir out of the water at the edge of the rocks nor in the creek itself so that even an old woman need not be troubled if she were sitting in a sheltered nook by the edge of a rock—for there was no fear of her being drowned! Dunmore stood out before me and Liúir too, like its watchdog, its crest covered with seagulls and cormorants resting at their ease; the Seanduine—Old Man Rock himself—was grinning beside them, his skull covered with a fleece of seaweed—though a person might say that it was high time for that same skull to be shaken and stripped by the mighty and insolent ocean waves that were forever crashing down upon it. Maol, or Baldie Bank, looked so peaceful and mild-tempered that you wouldn't think he ever did hurt or harm, though the old people said that it was on that rock the King of Spain's

177

ship was wrecked long ago. And that finished the vessel and all on board—God save those who hear the tale!

Out before me stood Dunquin—the fresh colour of summer on its fields and gardens—this was where I had spent my early days. Many the fine evening I was on top of that hill, Mount Eagle, when I was young and airy and with no responsibility whatsoever to carry. Away to the north stood the headland of Ceann Sratha and there also lay the mouth of Ferriter's Cove and Dún an Óir. Binn Diarmada appeared both triumphant and stately; the sunlight glistened brightly on its sides and on the deep scars the mighty ocean had wrought upon it. From Fiach to Barra Liath was one great sea harbour; it resembled a single sheet of glass and indeed, an observer might see it as a great city lying under a magic spell.

A sigh welled up from my heart and I said aloud: 'God! isn't it an odd person indeed who would be troubled in mind with so much beauty around him and all of it the work of the Creator's hand?'

I jumped with fright as a voice came from behind me.

'Isn't it time you were going home?' the voice said—it was Seán Eoghain who spoke.

'I daresay it is, Seán,' I told him, 'but to tell the truth I haven't much mind to do so.'

'That's no wonder, my poor woman,' said Seán. 'Everyone feels lonely after a death of a child.'

'Not child, Seán,' I said, 'but children.' I would have preferred any other topic of converstaion at that time and so as to change the subject I said. 'Look, Seán! There's Hy-Brasail to the north!'

'You devil you, where?' said Seán for he was a man with curses to burn. He turned on his heel.

'No doubt about it, but it's a lovely view on a summer afternoon,' he said. 'A person would take his oath that it's some enchanted land.'

'Yes, indeed,' I said. 'I often heard Eibhlís Sheáin say that she herself saw Hy-Brasail appearing in that very place one autumn evening while she was cutting furze on the Brow of Coum.'

'The devil sweep yourself and Eibhlís Sheáin,' Seán

replied in a humorous way that was meant for my good. 'And when you go to Hy-Brasail that you may never leave it! Get up and go home for yourself. 'Tis time for you to be off now!'

'You're right, I suppose,' I said, and I took up the stocking that lay beside me; indeed I hadn't much work done that afternoon.

It has been said that there is no joy in life without its own sorrow to accompany it. I thought I had finished with the woes of the world for those of my family who lived were now grown men. Muiris and Pádraig were fishing for themselves and Mícheál and Tomás were coming to maturity after them. Even if their father's health had failed they weren't depending on him; their uncle was giving them a hand and well able he was to do so.

Scattering and Sorrow

*Tomás dies accidentally — Pádraig and Cáit go to America
— My husband dies — Muiris, Eibhlín and Mícheál leave
me one after the other — Mícheál's poetry*

WHEN a person thinks his life is going smoothly then it
changes as if he were a cat's-paw of fate; that's a true
saying for it's exactly what happened to me, alas, in the
year 1920.

We had no turf on the Island that year; the fuel we
used was heather from the hill, and that was the fuel
I bought dearly! On the morning of Friday the 20th day
of April, Tomás and myself were up early. We had the
tea ready and no one else in the house had as yet risen.
While we were eating I told Tomás that Pádraig intended
going to America.

'Don't let it bother you!' he said. 'Isn't it time he
went?'

'It's a pity he won't stay with ye for another year,' I
said. 'Ye're too young to handle a currach and as the
proverb has it, "One year matures a child greatly."'

He looked at me across the table. A light shone in his
grey eyes; then he stretched out his right hand.

'Afraid you'll be hungry, mother?' he asked. 'Don't
be a bit in dread that this hand won't be able to put a
bite of food into your mouth!'

'I know that, but the hand is still soft and young,' I
said.

By the time we had the breakfast eaten the other
members of the family were getting up. Tomás stood in
the middle of the floor; he appeared to be pondering on
some subject, for he examined every inch of the house
carefully. Then he proceeded out the door. 'I won't go to

180

the hill today,' he said as he stood between the two door-jambs.

'The heather is too wet and we have enough inside for today,' I said. 'Let it hold over till tomorrow.'

He bounced out the door and that was the last time I saw him alive. When next I saw him he was calm and dead, laid out on a bier before me and the gentle bright hand he had stretched out so proudly to me in the morning was broken, bruised and lifeless.

It appears that when he left me that time in the morning he met other lads on their way to the hill to gather heather and he went off with them. The poor fellow was pulling a bush of heather when it gave way with him and he fell over the cliff top. He fell on his back pitching from rock to rock, each rock hundreds of feet above the sea until he crashed down at the bottom of the ravine. And may God save the hearers!

I knew nothing whatsoever about his being on the hill that day; I thought he was rambling around the neighbourhood with the other lads—until news of his death reached me. God save us, my life was then completely shattered. Fear and awe seized the heart of everyone for this was something that had never before happened on the Island and this multiplied everyone's terror. As far as I was concerned, no pen can describe what I suffered and endured. My son was dead; for the previous year his father had been keeping to the bed and when he heard the news the terrifying scream of sorrow he uttered will remain branded in my heart forever. The poor man thought that if he could only leave the bed he would be all right but even that much was beyond him.

That was my difficulty—how could I go away and leave my husband there in the pains of death? Tomás was gone to God but my husband was still alive and I realized that it would be flying in the face of the Almighty to leave the house without having someone to look after him. God granted me that much sense, praise be to Him forever, that I remained behind to give him a helping hand.

Two currachs and eight men had to go out to bring

back the body. When they came to the place where he was they were amazed to find that instead of his being hundreds of yards out in the broad ocean he was high up on a hollow smooth slippery detached stone barely the length and breadth of his body. There he was laid out as expertly and as calmly as if twelve women had tended him. No one knows how he landed on that table of stone with the blue sea all around him. No one except God alone.

When his body was brought back to the house the rest of the family was terrified except alone Muiris. He was more mature than the others. The neighbours had to take Cáit and Pádraig away from me because they were demented with shock. As for their unfortunate sick father, I didn't know the minute he'd drop dead. Remember, you who read this, that I was in a predicament if ever a poor woman was. The neighbours got such a fright that they were too terrified to approach me, all with the exception of two—Seán Eoghain and Máire Scanlan. Seán himself is dead now, God rest his soul and the souls of all the dead, but that same Seán—aye and God!—came to my relief on that sorrowful afternoon. There was hard work to be done and who would do it? That was the problem! I was only a mother and the job on hands was beyond me. I, who wouldn't like to see a simple cut had to set about the task; I had to wash and clean my fine young boy and lay him out in death. That task was before me and there was no way out of it. I hadn't a friend or relation beside me and I needed a heart of stone to be able to stand it.

I prayed to the Sacred Heart and to the Holy Mother to come and assist me! And indeed, dear reader, when I returned to the place where my son was, it could have been the body of a stranger, I felt my courage so strong and my heart so lightsome! But the task I had undertaken was too much for me; when I found my heart tightening I took the statue of the Virgin and placed it on the floor beside me and from that moment forward I confess that I was but an instrument in the hands of the Virgin and her only Son.

Muiris and his uncle, together with two others had gone

off to get what was needed for the wake. When they returned, Muiris was uneasy asking if he could blot out the English inscription on the breastplate of the coffin. This he succeeded in doing for the schoolmaster helped him and wrote it out again in Irish. Muiris was completely satisfied when he had done this. He then said:

'It's a great relief to my mind to know that you're the first corpse for hundreds of years to go into Ventry churchyard under an inscription in Irish.'

We found times upsetting and bothersome but God always opens a gap, for Tomás was barely six weeks buried when Father Seoirse Clune came to the Island on his holidays. I admit that it was God himself and Father Clune who gave me the first shred of comfort. Father Clune was with me every day for I had fluent Irish to give him; something better than that, he had sound advice and prime teaching to give me in return and that was a great help in healing a wounded heart. Scarcely a day passed that he wasn't with me and however sad I'd be on his arrival it seemed as if a ray of light accompanied him and that all my troubles would vanish. I was sorry when he left the Island, for he certainly helped me in great measure to forget my worldly troubles. This day, I wish him a long life in the service of God!

Six months after this my son Pádraig hoisted his sails and went off to America. There's no need for me to say that I was lonely after him but my hope in God was that I'd see him again some day. 'Better hope from a locked door than from a grave.' As soon as he had earned the passage-money Pádraig sent for his sister Cáit.

All these events were raining powerful blows on my heart, and barely five months after Cáit had gone, her father died—Lord have mercy on his soul. His heart was broken with sorrow and ill-health. His death was the worst blow I suffered and it left me poor and without anyone near me to offer me much assistance.

But while Muiris remained, I still had a man on my floor. He was an excellent son and one on whom I could depend completely. He was deeply attached to his country and to his native language and he never had any desire to leave Ireland. But that's not the way events turned out for he too had to take to the road like the others, his heart laden with sorrow.

As soon as he had turned the last sod on his father's grave he made ready to go. The day he went will remain forever in my memory because beyond all I had endured, nothing ever dealt me as crushing a blow as that day's parting with Muiris. The morning he left he was standing with his luggage and his papers on the table beside him. I was seated in the corner doing my best to be pleasant, but unknown to him I was watching him because he stood there as stiff as a poker with his two lips clamped together as if he were thinking. He rounded on me.

'Here!' he said handing me something wrapped in paper. I took it and opened it; it was the Irish flag.

'Yes,' he said again with a tremor in his voice, 'Put that away to keep in a place where neither moths nor flies can harm it! I have no business of it from this out.' Then he got a catch of emotion in his voice.

'Son, dear,' I said, 'this will do me more harm than good for it will only make me lonely.'

'No!' he said, and the words that jerked out of his mouth were all mixed up because of his emotion. 'You'll have it to welcome the Royal Prince of the Feast yet!'

However badly I felt, I had to laugh at him but this was, as they say, 'laughter from the teeth out.'

'You poor silly awkward gom,' I said. 'You'll have to put these ideas out of your head!'

'Before God,' he said, 'it's true for you. And isn't this a sad day for me!'

'God is mighty and He has a good Mother,' I told him. 'Gather your gear and have courage for there was never a tide flowed west but flowed east again.'

'Maybe in God it could happen,' he said and he held my hand in a grip of steel.

I followed him down to the slip; what with all the people making their way to the haven it was like a great funeral that day.

He promised me that if things went well with him I'd never want either by day or by night and that he'd return to me as soon as he had a fair amount of money put together. True, that talk gave me courage but I knew well that in the words of the proverb: 'The city has a broad entrance but a narrow exit.'

'My dear son,' I said. ''Twould be a bad place that wouldn't be better for you than this dreadful rock. Whatever way things go you'll be among your own equals. All around me here I see nothing on which a man can earn a living for here there's neither land nor property. I wouldn't like to make a cormorant of you, my son, and already too many are suffering misfortune. My own blessing and the blessing of God go with you. Follow your own road but heed me now, let nothing cross your path that'll lessen the love of God in your heart. Cherish your faith, avoid evil and always do good. A blessing go with you now and may God take you with him in safety.'

I was very uneasy in my mind until I got a letter from him.

Mícheál and Eibhlín were the last pair to leave me. Eibhlín was the youngest of all and I thought I'd never allow her go to America. At this time she was in Dublin in Seán O'Shea's house in Dundrum and I was completely content with that. She had nothing but love and respect for Seán, but alas, her brother Pádraig paid a visit home and nothing would satisfy him but to go up to Dublin and bring her back. He took her away with him when he was returning to America.

Then Mícheál was watching out for the chance to be off; he had no great mind to leave home but nevertheless, life was hard and he had nothing better to do. He too thought that if God left him his health he could put a fair share of money together and then come back home to me. A few days before he left the house he said:

'I wouldn't be a bit loath to leave, mother, if you'd promise me not to be lonely.'

'If I promised you that, son.' I told him, 'I'd promise you a lie; but I give you my word that I'll do my best not to be troubled.'

He was fairly satisfied then, although he was sad and heartbroken. The second day after that, he bade me good-bye, asked God to bless me and said:

'I hope, mother, that we'll be together again.'

'Maybe we will, boy,' I said, 'with God's help.'

Then he went out the door and faced down for the landing-slip. I was absolutely desolate when he was gone.

A few days later I was tidying the little odds and ends he had left behind when I came across a scrap of paper on which he had written the following verses:

Mother dear, don't weep for me,
Nor for the lost one intercede;
Lament the Virgin's shining Son
Your help in time of direst need.

Lament his beauteous royal brow,
His lime-white limbs that once were free;
Lament the pearl was shattered sore
On Calvary's hideous tree.

Herdsman Who gave us clerics fair,
To you we cry, dear Master,
Place hatred in our hearts for sin
The source of your disaster.

Bless thou myself and all my kin
At home or o'er the sea
And by the Holy Spirit's grace
Let not one stray from Thee.

For mother, Judgement Day shall come
When mocking lie dare not intrude—
You'll view our shining Saviour then,
King of the multitude.

By God's assistance, saints' and choirs',
I'll cross the raging tide,
And pleasant, sheltered, two as one
Together we'll abide.

Life Alone and Lonely

Story-telling to pass our nights — The night of the great gale — How five girls were drowned at the foot of Fahan — The girl whose hand was gripped

So the upshot of it all was that one by one the children left me and that I was left alone in a large empty house without a cow or a sheep, without a penny in my pocket, or a person to speak a word to me except a feeble old man drawing the 'blind pension'—Mícheál, my husband's brother, a man who had worked hard trying to help me and my family. He was the one who prepared them for work, as I have already explained, when their father was deprived of his health and the family was young. He was now without either a stranger or a kinsman to guide him. He'd get many people to accept him for his pension-money but it was very easy to treat him unfairly.

I kept turning over in my own mind what a great injustice it would be for me to wrong him at the end of his days. As yet, I was hardy and strong so the decision I came to was that if the two of us could remain on helping one another that that would be the best way out of our difficulty. I cast aside any thoughts I might have had and Mícheál and I remained together as brother and sister.

What a person reckons the worst thing that could possibly happen to him often turns out to be the very best; before long my son Mícheál returned from America and it was well for him that he had the house before him. 'It's an ill wind blows nobody good'—the hardship of the world was the cause of Mícheál's coming home and if he was sad I was delighted.

Often when the old man and myself were sitting half-lonely by the fireside with no one to make ins or outs on us he and I would begin to tell each other little stories so as to while away the night. He'd tell of the hardship he had endured and the frights he had got so often whilst out fishing.

'Do you remember the night of the great gale?' he asked me one night.

'I remember it well,' I said. 'It was a dreadful night.'

'That afternoon was very fine,' he went on, 'and all the little boats went out fishing. But it wasn't long until the night became squally and there was a high sea and a ground swell with the result that the little currachs were unable to come ashore. There were eight currachs in all and they were filled with fish. The fishermen didn't know what best to do; some of them advised heading south for Ventry Harbour. The night was dark and it seemed as if the wind would blow very strongly. They hoisted their sails and made off towards the south. Up to this, the bay was calm and they didn't feel the journey to Ventry; however, the other Islanders spent a very restless night thinking of their own people in danger.

'The following morning was neither calm nor quiet; a gale blew from the west and south with such force as would give a ship all it could do to weather it. At ten o'clock in the morning someone spied one of the little boats rounding Slea Head to the south and he shouted at the top of his voice that the boats were coming. God of Miracles! such terror and confusion as there was then! Every woman and child, aye and every man, young and old were gathered south at the Point, some of them trembling from head to foot with terror. There was real horror, deeply expressed in cries of grief and beating of hands as the cliffside around answered with the lonely echoes of '*Ochón-ó.*' Then Nell Mhicil, the oldest woman on the Island at that time, began to speak.

'"Stop your wailing," she said. "Don't you know that God prefers prayers to tears?" and she told us to go down on our knees and she began to recite the Stanza of Saint Michael as a protection against drowning:

189

Crossing over the deep ford,
O King of Patience, place your hand on them
For fear of the blow of the great wave.
Mary, watch them! Don't abandon them!

'I had never heard that prayer before nor have I heard it since. Like a flock of black crows, one following the other, the boats drew near, each without a mast or sail left untattered by the gale. And we never got up from our knees until the last currach had reached the Mouth of the Strand.

'The poor men were emotionally drained and exhausted but the Islanders made light of that for they were well used to such experiences. For the week that followed the people had no topic of conversation on road or on pathway but how well the men had steered through The Old Man's Sound on that dreadful day.'

'Mícheál, have you ever heard how the five girls were drowned at the foot of Fahan long ago?'

'No!' Mícheál said, placing a live coal of fire on his pipe.

'At that time custom forbade anyone to go to the strand on Whit Monday or to put to sea in a boat on Whit Sunday. However, there were five young girls in the parish of Ventry at that time; they were the pick of the parish, and again none of their people had another daughter except these. They decided to go picking *báirneachs* and they paid no heed to the fact that it was Whit Monday. An aunt of one of the girls was married in Fahan and living in a house above the sea and they thought they could do no better than have a day of enjoyment. So off they went in a band and they never stopped until they reached the aunt's house; she was surprised to see them coming and asked them where they were off to.

'"To the strand," they said. "We won't make much delay. Have the potatoes boiled before us when we come back!"

190

'They left her and went away back towards the beach and the aunt started to put down the potatoes to boil. When they were boiled she told one of the children to go out and see if the girls were coming.

'"They're not coming yet," the child said. "They're on the cliff-top dancing."

'When the aunt thought that they were a long time coming she went out herself and there they were still, dancing a four-hand reel with the fifth girl playing for them. But they were *not* coming and they never came afterwards, for at the exact time she saw them dancing, God save us! they were drowned.

'It's said that a great number of people saw a dreadful sign on that same day. Two women from Dunquin were north in Tonakilly picking *báirneachs*, an old woman and a newly-married woman who was pregnant. After going down to the beach, the old woman didn't fancy having the young woman taking any risk so she told her to remain above at the foot of the stile and that she herself would go down. The young woman did as she was told; she was sitting down looking out to sea and after a short time she saw an almighty huge wave rising at the approach to the beach. She cried out to the woman below:

'"For God's sake, run or you'll be drowned!"

'The other woman ran in time but only barely so. The pair had just crossed above the stile and had caught a firm grip of a tall pointed protruding stone when the destructive wave ran right over them, tearing at the stones and the rocks that lay in its path. Only that the two women had kept a grip on the rock they'd have been drowned. When they came to the cliff-top they saw the same terrible wave moving southward and away from them and they got the impression that there was a man sitting on its crest with a red cap on his head.

'Other people also saw the same sight and they kept watching the wave until it had passed Slea Head and had moved away to the south. This was the same wave that had caught up with those five girls and swept them off.'

'It was an appalling disaster and one that cast a gloom over the people of the entire parish. Four of the finest

Máire's in Ireland and a Máighréad Bhán! From that day forward I don't think that anyone from that locality ever went down to the beach picking *báirneachs* on Whit Monday—nor on Whit Saturday but as little.'

'That's a marvellous story,' Mícheál said poking some glowing embers out of the fire with the tongs.

'My dear man, things as wonderful as that happen,' I told him.

'Wasn't the story of the girl whose hand was gripped by the man—it happened somewhere near the same locality—just as wonderful?' Mícheál wanted to know.

'How was that?' I asked and I was truly delighted because I simply loved odd stories of that nature. I had that streak in my character ever since I was a child.

'Four girls from Kilvickadownig—grand girls they were—went off one fine autumn evening picking *báirneachs*. At that time of year limpets are given to slithering —swimming across the rocks in the amber light of sunset. The girls were picking and collecting what are called 'fairy barnacles' and one of them, Eibhlín O'Sullivan, was down in a little spot where a pool of sea-water had lodged. She saw some *báirneachs* moving under the mouth of the stone beside her so she bent down and thrust in her hand; but if she did, another hand gripped hers and she couldn't pull out her hand. She called out to the others and when they came, they could not move the hand either so they were forced to leave Eibhlín behind them and, almost at their last gasp, go and tell her people that she was in danger of being drowned.

'The hand inside held Eibhlín's hand in a deathlike grip until the tide had flowed three yards above her on the beach. Then it released its hold. When her people came on the scene she was completely knocked out with shock. People said it was a crab had caught her but she never admitted herself that it was.'

'Mícheál, was that the girl to whom the ship's captain offered ten pounds for a couple of locks of her hair?'

'The exact same girl!'

'I wonder, Mícheál, what business would the silly clown have of her hair?'

'He wanted it, girl, to make a wig of it!'

That's how myself and the poor blind man passed away the time. Sometimes the going was easy; at other times it was hard.

Fireside Tales

Learners of Irish on the Island — The woman who fell over the cliff — The dancer in the night — The piper of the cliff — Grey Bríghde and how she buried the last member of her family

DURING that period, a great number of strangers kept coming to the Island from time to time and they'd often spend a long while with us. While they were with me I hadn't a scrap of worry for it was a great ease to my heart to chat with them and to spout out Irish! I found great satisfaction in their coming and going every evening. I could say that I was a teacher to them and I'd often give a little snap at them when they'd be stupid, but you can believe every word I say, I hadn't to snap a second time. They had the word, or the question, I wanted, on the tips of their tongues the following evening.

There were two strangers here, and they'd seldom let a day pass without paying us a visit. They came in to see me one evening and to tell the truth they were very welcome on that occasion. It was raining heavily outside, but I had a fine glowing fire before them because I was expecting them. Their names were Seán and Séamas but I can't recall their surnames. I never called Seán anything but Long John; he hadn't much Irish but the other man had it fair enough. For the very reason that Seán hadn't Irish I did my utmost to help him and almost every night I had a tale or a stanza for him.

We were seated comfortably by the fireside; I asked Seán if he had been on the hill that day.

'I was at the Tower,' he said. 'Isn't there a fine view from there!'

'Did you go as far as the Haven of the Little Cliff?' I asked.

'No!' he answered, 'but I was there the other day and it's a high and eerie kind of place.'

'What would you say if I told you that a woman fell down there and wasn't killed?'

'I wouldn't believe it,' Seán said, 'I wouldn't believe that a dog could fall down there and not lose its life.'

'I give you my solemn word, Seán, that you'd be making a mistake in that! A woman fell down there and she wasn't killed either!'

'Tell us the story, Peig,' he said.

I wet my lips, settled myself on the stool in the corner and braced myself for talking.

'Yes, my dear men,' I began, 'there were two women on this Island at the time of my arrival here, Moll and Máire Kearney. One fine evening they went off cutting cliff grass to the Haven of the Little Cliff—this was because there was a scarcity of oats that year. They were standing on a wide patch in the middle of the cliff—a place where once an eagle had its nest. The grass on that sod was fine and long because even a goat couldn't get at it, but at that time the pair of women were as agile as any goat. It so happened that Moll met with some mishap and fell over the cliff edge and every despairing screech she uttered while tumbling down drew echoes from the cliffside.

'When Máire Kearney saw this appalling sight—her dear friend Moll, pitching down—she almost went clean out of her mind. She never knew how she got to the top of the cliff nor did she look back over her shoulder until she had passed east through the Dead Man's Bed. She heard Moll calling her but the poor woman thought, and I wouldn't blame her in the least for it, that it was Moll's ghost was there. However fast she walked, Moll kept gaining ground so that when Máire came to Maumna-lacken she could go no further for the poor woman was worn out by the hard going. "Whether you're dead or alive," Máire said to herself, "I can't move one other step. And anyway, I'm within sight of the people now."

'She wasn't long seated when Moll arrived. Máire looked at her in between the two eyes.

195

'"Divine God!" she asked, "are you dead or alive?"

'"Alive, to be sure," Moll answered. "Why didn't you wait for me when I called you?"

'"My dear woman," Máire answered, "how could I wait for you when I thought you were in the other world?"

'"There isn't a whack the matter with me," said Máire, "but my bones are bruised. For God's sake, don't open your mouth about this to anyone or I'll be a right laughin'-stock."

'But alas! Máire had only barely landed home when the story was out of her beak.'

'God bless us!' said Seán, 'how did the woman survive?'

'Ould Nick himself wouldn't kill the women who lived then, Seán,' I told him. 'You can take it, lad, that it wasn't a baba's skin that covered the soles of their feet but skin as tough as the hide of the White-Loined Cow of legend, for those women were as hardy and as strong as any man! But that's not the way with the women nowadays—they couldn't hold candlelight to those I've mentioned and may God grant eternal life to the souls of those who are gone.'

'I met Moll a week afterwards and I asked her if she was terrified, or was everything that Máire Kearney had said about her true.

'"It is true, child, but I didn't get time to be frightened. But, indeed, as the man said long ago if a miss wasn't as good as a mile I was done for. A clump of thrift stopped me after I had fallen a long way down, but I was a deal more frightened by the pooka I saw long ago."

'"You saw him, Moll?"

'"If I didn't see him, I heard him!" she said. "At that time we had a habit of spinning until all hours of the night. One woman would be spinning and another carding. The woman I had carding was from Dunquin; she was due to go home the following day and as it was a Sunday she was in a hurry to finish up the work. But sleep was getting the upper hand of me," said Moll, "and I couldn't do much to help her. She started singing a tune called—'The Little Red Fox' and she had barely started the tune when the dancer began tapping out the rhythm on the flagstone outside the door. Grey Bríghde cocked her ear.

"'Moll,' she asked me, 'do you hear anything?'

"'God's truth, I hear it,' I said.

"Bríghde gave one buck-jump up from the spinning-wheel and landed right inside Diarmaid, this man of mine, who was sleeping in a high bed in the corner. Off with me in after her and neither one nor the other of us took off a stitch of clothes that night. Bríghde went home the following day, and from that day to this she never came to spin to this Island.'"

'Who on earth was dancing on the flagstone of the doorway at that ungodly hour of the night?' Seán asked me.

'How do I know, man?' I said. 'Moll herself didn't know but as little. I daresay it was a ghost—if such things exist.'

'Is it true that things like that move around among the living?' Seán asked me.

'People say so,' I said. 'I remember the time the people would gather for a dancing session on the Moor. The piper they had as musician was called "The Hairy Piper" because he had a long mop of heavy grey hair. An O'Sullivan man lived in the Coum at that time and he was an outstanding dancer with a tremendous turn for music. One Saturday evening after dinner he arrived to the Moor but there was neither music nor dancing there before him because the unfortunate piper was sick. Tomás O'Sullivan was greatly put out; he dug his two hands into his britches pockets and faced west again for the Coum. The evening was very fine and the sea was calm and by this time the tide had fully ebbed. When he was west of the top of Pigeons' Cove, he thought he heard music below him so he looked down over the cliff-edge and saw a piper sitting on a fine level flagstone near the verge of the ebbed tide. The piper was playing softly and sweetly; as the sun set the music stirred O'Sullivan's heart so down he went along a narrow dangerous foot-path and never stopped until he stood directly in front of the piper. The instant he stood there the piper stopped playing. Then, Tomás, addressing him boldly, for at that moment he thought the other was a mortal man, said "Play me a turn, please! I'd like to do a couple of steps of dancing."

'The piper started playing and he never stopped until Tomás was completely satisfied.

'"Thanks a thousand!" Tomás said, "you're the finest piper that ever put a pipe to his lips."

'Without saying as much as one word the piper placed his pipes in his bag. Tomás left him there—the man was gazing north-west towards the Grey Crest—and never looked back until he reached the cliff-top. When he looked down in the direction of the flagstone he couldn't see trace nor tidings of the piper.

'Tomás's feet and hands began to tremble with terror and he spent six long months on the flat of his back in bed.'

'But death never paid him a call!' Seán said.

'Dickens a call, indeed! Although many people said that that was what the piper was foreshowing.'

'Brighde, whom I have already mentioned, was a sister to Tomás's father. She suffered great trouble and distress at the start of her days. She was married in the Coum in Famine Times; eight in family she had, but indeed, not one of them survived. Hunger killed some of them—not all of them to be sure, but what followed the hunger, God between us and all harm. Brighde had buried seven of the family and their father, and all she had left alive then was herself and her eldest daughter, the loveliest and finest girl seen in Kerry for generations. To crown her misfortune, God save us, the daughter died too.

'That was no great novelty in those days; Brighde had no one to give her a helping hand because all the people were dispirited so she herself had to carry her daughter's body to the graveyard—a bitter experience for the poor woman. She got a súgán rope and tied it around the daughter's waist; then she tied the rope around her own waist and placed the dead daughter's two hands on her own shoulders from behind. That's how she brought the corpse to Ballinahow graveyard, walking and resting, every second turn.

'A woman from Ballinglanna saw her passing—her name was Nóra Landers. "May God look down on you, Bríghde," she said in her own mind, "your heart is crushed this day and you're played out with hunger. If only I could do something for you!"

'She turned into her room and brought out six potatoes from a handful of seed potatoes she had stored; she put the potatoes roasting under live embers so that she'd have them ready when Bríghdín would be passing back again.

'When Bríghde reached the churchyard with her load, she hadn't the strength to open the grave; four men from Ballinahow arrived and covered the daughter for her with sods of earth.

'As soon as the last sod was on the grave, Bríghde cried out in a loud voice:

'"Sleep peacefully in eternal rest, beloved family and gentle husband! There's no fear that you'll ever awaken until the ocean pours from the north and the dark raven turns snow white. Have no fear now, dear ones, that you will ever again suffer hunger or thirst. You have plenty in the Stream of Glory to quench your thirst this day. I leave you now to rest in the grace of God until the angel sounds his trumpet on Judgement Day."

'Bríghde was right, for a sod hasn't been turned on that grave ever since. She faced for home but, if she did, Nóra stood before her on the road.

'"Come in with me, poor Bríghde," she said. "You have the evening long for walking west."

'"Wisha, Nóra, I have no business walking west any more for what I owned of the west I've buried in God's ground this day."

'"Never mind that, Bríghde! Come in; I have a fistful of potatoes under the embers for you. Come on in and eat them and it'll give you courage for the long road."

'"God grant you never know trouble like mine!"

'Bríghde sat by the fire and Nóra brought her a drop of milk and put the roast potatoes before her. Bríghde caught one of the potatoes in her hand and said in a loud voice: "Thanks be to God that it isn't you for a potato I have left in Ballinahow."

'That drew a tear from Nóra's eye for she knew right well that Bríghde needed the potatoes at that time.

'Bríghde went home but she didn't settle down there for long for her house was set on fire and it was burned to the ground. That left Bríghde without house, relatives, husband or family so she was forced into spending a night here and a night there. She was very skilful at spinning flax and wool; that meant that she never lacked work, for people were, as the saying goes, "tearing her from each other." She lived to be ninety years of age.'

'You're a wonderful storyteller,' Seán said. 'It's extraordinary the number of fine tales you have. But I daresay, Peig, it's time now to "hit the sop!"'

'It is,' I answered. 'And as the man said, "Everyone gets a second chance and Old Ireland will yet be free!"'

Adventures of Mine

Mad for tobacco! — The pup takes my short pipe — The Charm of the Stitch and how it was first done — The dog that bit my leg — Myself and the doctor who spoke English

IN this locality there was another stranger called Pádraig Walsh and he'd often visit me just like the others. Pádraig was a great man for fun and company and I'd be lonesome any night he wouldn't turn up at the house. Whenever he'd go to Dunquin, on his return he'd nearly always have some humorous yarn to tell me and when he'd arrive to pass away part of the night with us we wouldn't be one bit lonely. This day the weather was very fine and Pádraig went into the mainland for he was always a man who liked to be on the sea.

'I wonder,' I said to Mícheál, 'will our gay friend, Pádraig, pay us a visit tonight?'

'To be sure he will, with God's help,' said Mícheál, and he'll have a great deal of news after returning from Dunquin.' Then Mícheál went off out for himself.

He wasn't long gone when I got a mind for a puff of the pipe. I think that there's a curse down on top of anyone with a mind for tobacco or snuff and this is especially true of an Island like this, because often a person has no way of getting tobacco, nor indeed a number of other articles as well. I had my old clay pipe ready and God knows, that same old pipe was every day as ancient as the old tower on top of the hill and was well-branded with its trade too. Believe you me, dear reader, that this was so!

I put the pipe down out of my hands on the flagstone of the hearth and off I went foraging for the smallest particle of tobacco to put into it but I wasn't finding any and the craving inside me was getting worse. Man dear, I

201

searched and researched every corner and hole where I'd leave a bit of 'baccy out of my hand but devil a scrap did I find. With the crazy mind *he* had for tobacco Tigeen was never in such a predicament as I was at that moment.

What did I do but go to the tea canister so as to put a grain of tea into my clay pipe. But when I came back to the flagstone my little pipe wasn't there before me!

'Almighty Father!' I said to myself. 'What's wrong with me today? Without one word of a lie 'baccy fever has a grip of me. I'd swear by all the brindled bibles of the Pope that I left my pipe down on the flagstone when I went searching for the tobacco. And see now, that flagstone is as clear as a crystal and clean as well without a trace of a dúdeen! If the dead had any reason to play jokes on me . . . but what cause of complaint would they have with me? Hadn't they a great mind for tobacco when they were alive, as I am now?'

My word, dear reader, I felt as tormented as a roast herring. The grain of tea in the hollow of my hand, my head in the air, and I going around the floor like a drunken man, but my little short-stemmed pipe was nowhere to be found!

Out I went onto the passageway to see if I'd find any provision. I looked down towards the lower end of the yard and there was that trickster of a puppy of ours making a knocking noise with something he was chewing. I went down towards him and what had he but my little pipe and it was almost ground down to powder under his teeth.

'The curse of Mushera Mountain down on top of you, you rascal,' I said, 'if you aren't the boyo who's knocking tally-ho out of my pipe after all my searching!'

He cocked an ear for he knew well that he had played the robber.

When I came back, Mícheál had returned to the house and you can be certain that I had a smoke of tobacco then! I thought it the height of misfortune ever to have put the stem of a pipe into my mouth, but then again, I daresay that everyone has his own weakness.

I was sitting there, sending a cloud of smoke out of the

pipe, and what should I see coming in the door but our
big belter of a cat with one of Máire's chickens—Máire
is a next-door neighbour—in his jaws. He gave me a start
for I was full sure that Máire would be raging with me if
she knew that it was my cat had killed the chicken. I
chased after the cat calling out 'Pusheen! Pusheen!' in
the hope that he'd drop the chicken. The big long chalk
pipe was dancing in my mouth as I had only two teeth
left with which to grip it and this grip I held until I
reached the door. But alas, I was so taken up with the
cat that I forgot to steady the pipe with my hand so down
it fell on the threshold stone and was broken into flitters.
When Mícheál saw it in pieces his comment was:

'Wisha, that's instead of some harm to your health, my good woman!'

Away goes the cat and he made a right job of the chicken and a second chicken after that, and if I hadn't told Seán—Máire's husband—to watch out for his chickens the brindled cat wouldn't have left one of them in the land of the living. But the robber didn't succeed in getting his teeth into any more of them!

With the fall of night Pádraig and his companions walked in the door.

'Welcome, son!' I said to him.

'God spare you the health,' Pádraig answered.

'You've a lot of stories after the day?'

'Not many, indeed,' Pádraig said. 'Maybe you have a story yourself.'

''Pon my soul, you'd have a right story if you were watching me today!'

'What was wrong with you, Peig?' Pádraig wanted to know.

''Baccy daftness, boy, if ever an old woman had it.'

'You haven't such a mind for it, Peig, have you?'

'I don't think that there's another old woman alive who has more mind for tobacco that I have,' I said, and I started telling him the story of the pipe. And if they didn't enjoy it, it isn't day yet.

'Peig, where's Mícheál?' Pádraig asked.

'In bed! Bad cess to it, but he got a gripe in his guts! He isn't getting his health this while back, the poor man.'

'Can anything be done for him?' Pádraig asked.

'Not a thing! Unless the Charm of the Stitch would do him any good,' I replied.

'You think it would?' Pádraig asked.

'I often heard that whoever it was worked on, got relief.'

'No wonder it's good so,' Pádraig said.

'God's Mother has goodness and cures through the powers of her Glorious Son,' I said. ''Twas she put that round of words together first. And this is how it happened:

'Our Blessed Mother and her only Son were going on a long journey. He was six years of age, the road was too much for them and they were exhausted. They met no house where they could get shelter until morning, but at last they spied a little house some distance away from them. As the hour was getting late they quickened their pace; they reached the house and on going in, found only the housewife before them. The Virgin asked in a kindly tone to be allowed stay for the night as they were worn out from the long road.

'"No room for travelling people in this house," the housewife said in a rude tone of voice.

'As the Virgin and her little Son were going out the door whom should they meet coming in but the good man-of-the-house.

'"God be with you, travelling people!" he said.

'"The same to you, son!" the Virgin answered.

'"It's late now," he said. "Come on in with me."

'"We were in your house already, my decent man," the Virgin said, "and your wife told us that she had no room for people like us."

'"And I say she has!" the man said. "And no thanks to her either."

'They turned back with him; when the woman saw them again she was overcome with a fit of rage at her husband.

'"Give these travelling people food and drink," he told her in a kindly tone.

'"Give it to them yourself, if you think they'll be a long time hungry," she said with a rasp to her voice.

'They were like this clipping and quarrelling until bedtime. Then, because his angry wife wouldn't give him bedclothes, the man of the house put the child lying down on some flax tow. Even after they had gone to bed the arrogant woman never slackened in her abuse.

'"Isn't it a crying shame, my dear Son, that such a woman is married to a fine decent man," Mary said.

'"No cure for it, Mother, but to take the good man out of the way!"

'"That's a pity, Son—a man as good as him."

'With that, death gripped the man-of-the-house. He cried out: "God have mercy on me, I'm finished!" The pain was increasing and in the end neither Mary nor the child Jesus troubled the housewife, but her own husband.

'"Dearest Son," the Virgin said, "the good man's pain is worrying me. It's a great pity to have him in that plight, so rise up and do good!"

'"Rise up yourself, Mother, and *I* will do the good."

'Mary, the Mother of God, rose up and went to the bed on which the sick man was lying; she put her own palm and the palm of the Infant on the spot where the pain was, saying:

> *An arrogant wife has a meek husband*
> *Who put the body of Christ lying on flax tow;*
> *The palm of Mary and of her Son to the colic,*
> *In the name of the Father and of the Son and of*
> *the Holy Ghost.*

'The pain went away at once and the man was as well as ever he was.'

'Wouldn't you chance it, Peig?' Pádraig asked.

'I might as well. Come with me.'

Pádraig rose up from the chair and the two of us went upstairs. When we entered the bedroom where the sick man lay, I got a drop of holy water and shook it on a scrap of wadding. Then we went on our knees and I applied the wadding to the place where the pain was and recited the Charm of the Stitch. Pádraig was watching me carefully.

Before very long the sick man sneezed.

'May God help us!' I said, 'he's better.'

'I don't know that he is,' Pádraig said.

'He has every appearance of it!' I said. 'Dead men don't sneeze!'

Shortly after that Mícheál got out of bed and went up to the fireside; the people in the kitchen were astonished to lay eyes on the man, who, a couple of hours before, was on his way to Kingdom Come.

'You were right, Peig, when you said that the Mother of God through the power of her only Son, has goodness and cures,' Pádraig said.

'It is true,' I said, 'that He never refused her intercession. Praise and thanks a hundredfold in the heavens to His holy name!'

Mícheál was sitting on the chair humming away like he always was.

'Is that bout of pain gone now?' Pádraig asked him.

''Tis, thank God,' said Mícheál.

'The old woman is good!' Pádraig went on.

'She's good to me at any rate,' he said.

'I suppose you often got an attack of pain yourself, Peig?'—this from Pádraig.

'My body is swollen with those same pains—and that's one sure fact! Although I never suffered a more bitter nor a worse pain than when a dog took a bite out of my leg a long time ago. I thought that the pain would drive me out of my mind but the owner of the dog had little pity for me. He wouldn't kill the animal even if it had devoured half of my body! My leg was very sore and many people said that the wound would never heal until such time as the dog was done away with. The woman I was then working with said: "The doctor is coming up the road, so go before him to the crossroads and maybe he'll give you some prescription."

'I was barely able to reach the crossroads but anyway, I was there before the doctor. He kind of knew me and he asked me what had happened me. I told him that a dog had taken a bite out of my leg.

'"Take off the bandage till I see it," he said in English. When he looked at my leg: "The divil ate you!" he said.

He was a wild cross man and the look he'd give you was worse than a blow of a fist from another person.

'"Who owns the dog?" he asked.

'I told him that the dog belonged to Micil Ph'lib. He was on friendly terms with Micil so he didn't fancy the idea of doing away with the dog. He told me to stoop my leg with lukewarm water and soap.

'"That you may get the last stooping yourself, before long, you half-wit,"' I said.

'He left me and travelled off to the north, but dickens a home I came but rambled away up to Micil Ph'lib. There was no one in the house but himself.

'"What's up with you, now?" he asked.

'"I was talking to the doctor and he told me to tell you that if you hadn't the dog dead by the time he was back from the north, he'd send out two policemen to shoot him."

'I had belied the doctor, but I didn't care so long as my leg got better.

'Within ten minutes I heard Donnchadh, Micil's son, calling the dog.

'When the doctor arrived back from the north the dog had been hung from a tree in the garden. Donnchadh went to meet him so as to get satisfaction. Then the doctor was in a right tear; he fired every devil in hell after me but I didn't give a hang about him. My leg healed but until the day he died I didn't like the idea of meeting the doctor for fear he'd give me a telling-off.

'But he finally got me in a tight corner. He was coming to the Island cutting the children for "the pox" so all the women used gather into the schoolhouse—each with her own child. Anyhow, I was there with my son, Muiris, who was twelve months old at the time. The doctor was below at the table with the schoolmaster and he was calling out the names from a list. When he called my name in English I answered him and he asked me what age the child was. *Erra,* my dear man, it has always been said that even the parish priest can make a slip of the tongue and I made a slip too, because instead of saying "Twelve months" in Irish, I said "Twelve years" in English! When he heard this answer he flew into a dreadful rage and up he comes to me with this mad light blazing in his eyes. It was then I realized that I had made a right mistake.

'"Excuse me, doctor, it was a slip of the tongue!" I said in Irish, but to be sure, he didn't understand what I said. The teacher told him to have patience and that I was right.

'"She is not right!" he said. "She's jeering at me!

She belied me some time ago but she won't do it a second time."

'He was standing right over me by this time with an angry look on his face. Terrified as I was, I couldn't help laughing.

'"Doctor," I said, "you're one beautiful man, God bless you, except for the two eyes in your head. Upon my soul, they'd terrify the bravest man who ever lived."

'The teacher laughed, and the doctor himself had to laugh too—when he understood what I had said. He turned on his heel and walked back down to the table.'

The Last Chapter

IT has always been said that the last loss is the hardest to bear and it's only a short time ago that I got word about my son, Pádraig, who died in the States. If a woman like me has ever been born and has gone through the same share of the troubles of this world as I have, you may be certain that she has had enough to contend with. I have dragged my way through life suffering torment and sorrow and it's little comfort I knew during the whole of my days. But it's true that there is no cure for sorrow but to kill it with patience!

All my life too, I did my own small share for the Irish language. As I have already set down, a great number of strangers arrived on the Island from time to time and among them were Léan Connellan, a lovable girl who gave me great help in this work, and that noble soul Máire Kennedy whose name has long been held in esteem among the Irish people. If it weren't for Máire I'd have taken down to the grave all I have written here.

I gave every help to those who were learning Irish. Now I'm at the end of my days, and I suppose that never again will there be an old woman as Irish as me on this Island. What I put before me was to undertake the work before I died and that I'd have that satisfaction in my mind before my bones were laid under the green sod. I tried to write this story in the simplest possible way in which it could be read and understood—just as if I were telling it to the neighbouring children round the fireside. And I wasn't hard on any of my neighbours either; they gave me all the help they could. If they had their faults, I had mine. We passed our lives together peacefully and lovingly and on the hill or in the garden we gave one another a helping hand. If I was caught in a pinch all I had to do was to run for one of the neighbours and that tided me over until God came to my assistance. We spent our lives helping each other.

We were poor people who knew nothing about riches or the luxuries of life. We accepted the kind of life that was ours and never wished for any other. God, praise be to Him forever, gave us His assistance. We often noticed that the High and Holy Master was favourable to us because 'twas many a squall and storm of wind caught our people on the sea where there was no escape except through His power. Often they won the reward of their labours; often they did not.

Almost everyone I have mentioned in this story is dead, except myself alone, and before very long I'll travel that same road. I didn't bother putting down anything that hadn't to do with the tale but simply wrote down everything that interested me.

I'm old now, and every day I'm on the watch-out for the messenger from the life that I have no mind to enter, but I thank God that I can say that I am not ashamed to lift up my hand because my hand never harmed a neighbour. The most of my life, I've spent it on this lonely rock in the middle of the great sea. There's a great deal of pleasantry and hardship in the life of a person who lives on an island like this that no one knows about except one who has lived here—going to bed at night with little food and rising again at the first chirp of the sparrow, then harrowing away with the world and maybe having no life worth talking about after doing our very best.

We wouldn't have minded the hardship of life, however, but for the fact that death was gathering his strength behind it. But that rascal too has to get what's due to him.

I remember well when I was trying to work while at the same time the heart in my breast was broken by sorrow, that I'd turn my thoughts on Mary and on the Lord, and on the life of hardship *they* endured. I knew that it was my duty to imitate them and to bear my cross in patience. Often I'd take my little canvas sheet and face for the hill for a small amount of turf and on the road home the weight on my heart would have lifted. God's Son and His Glorious Mother are true friends!

I remember when I was young, when Cáit-Jim and myself were girls, playing on the bank of the river, gathering flowers in the fields, or going to school side by side. Look at me today, an old grey woman with hardly a tooth in my head!

Old as I am, there's a great deal more in my head that I can't write down here. I did my best to give an accurate account of the people I knew, so that we'd be remembered when we had moved on into eternity. People will yet walk above our heads; it could even happen that they'd walk into the graveyard where I'll be lying but people like us will never again be there. We'll be stretched out quietly—and the old world will have vanished.

I'm thankful to Máire Kennedy and to Léan Connellan who kept after me and helped me to finish this task. I hope that we'll meet again in the Kingdom of Heaven. May God grant us that blessing and may He grant it too to those who read these lines!

> *God's blessing on you, manuscript,*
> *My blessing too, on those who see it,*
> *Good luck attend my native land,*
> *God strengthen those who strive to free it!*

The Great Blasket,
The Feast of the Assumption,
1935.